C000244022

Race and Faith:
The Deafening Silence

Race and Faith:
The Deafening Silence

Trevor Phillips

with commentaries from

David Goodhart and Jon Gower Davies

First Published June 2016

© Civitas 2016
55 Tufton Street
London SW1P 3QL

email: books@civitas.org.uk

All rights reserved

ISBN 978-1-906837-79-2

Independence: Civitas: Institute for the Study of Civil Society is a registered educational charity (No. 1085494) and a company limited by guarantee (No. 04023541). Civitas is financed from a variety of private sources to avoid over-reliance on any single or small group of donors.

All publications are independently refereed. All the Institute's publications seek to further its objective of promoting the advancement of learning. The views expressed are those of the authors, not of the Institute, as is responsibility for data and content.

Designed and typeset by
lukejefford.com

Printed in Great Britain by
4edge Limited, Essex

Contents

Authors

Trevor Phillips is a writer and television producer. He is the chair of Green Park Diversity Analytics, and the deputy chair of the board of the National Equality Standard. He was the founding chair of the Equality and Human Rights Commission. He is the president of the John Lewis Partnership Council; the chair of the Workers' Educational Association; the vice-chair of the New York-based Center for Talent Innovation; a Fellow of the Migration Policy Institute (Washington DC) and of Imperial College London. He is the co-author (with Mike Phillips) of *Windrush: The Irresistible Rise of Multiracial Britain*.

David Goodhart is the founder editor of *Prospect* magazine, former director of the Demos think tank and author of *The British Dream: Successes and Failures of Post-War Immigration*. He is currently director of the Integration Hub (integrationhub.net) and head of the Demography, Immigration and Integration Unit at Policy Exchange.

Jon Gower Davies retired from the University of Newcastle in 1997, where he lectured first in the Social Studies Department, and then in the Department of Religious Studies, of which he was head. For 20 years he was a Labour councillor on Newcastle City Council. He is the author and editor of books and articles on a wide range of topics, including *Bonfires on the Ice: The multicultural harrying of Britain* (2007), *In Search of the Moderate Muslim* (2009), *A New Inquisition: religious persecution in Britain today* (2010) and *Small Corroding Words: The slighting of Great Britain by the EHRC* (2011).

Race and Faith: The Deafening Silence

Trevor Phillips

Britain is not a racist nation. But it is a society with a deep sensitivity to the dangers posed by ethnic and cultural difference. So touchy have we British become that we even find speaking of these topics difficult. Yet we live in a world beset by tribal and religious strife, which affect people living under every kind of political system. Both of the world's largest nations, democratic India and communist China, wrestle with troublesome ethnic conflicts. Sunni and Shia theocracies glare at one another across the Middle East.

Even our close cousins in the United States are mired in chronic culture wars. *Time* magazine's longtime star columnist, Joe Klein, opened 2016 by declaring that in this year's presidential election campaigns, 'race and tribe trump economics'.[1] One way or another, identity differences are a preoccupation across the modern world.

Islamist terrorism is now firmly camped on our own European shores. There are periodic outcries in the mainstream media about examples of individual racial or religious discrimination. Yet the evident distaste amongst European elites – particularly those in Britain – for any serious debate about the consequences of our growing ethnocultural diversity feels like a glaring exception to the global debate.

1

By and large, our nation is complacent about its ability to manage its own diversity; our opinion-formers watch events in the USA and on the continent with detachment, and congratulate themselves on the perception that there is no longer a substantial anti-immigrant or nativist party active in British politics. Integration is not a priority topic of discussion amongst the British political and media classes. This smugness, mistaken as it is, can be explained, given our historical success in this area.

For over half a millennium, the British have successfully managed ethnocultural diversity by what might be called a process of *organic integration*. The combination of a core set of values and behaviours, a habit of toleration for cultural difference or eccentricity, and a preference for the gradual absorption of new traditions has always provided both stability and resilience in our society. The two essential ingredients of this process are confidence in our existing values, and time for the process to work. In the 21st century, these qualities are both in short supply.

Today, more different groups of very different people are arriving in Britain in larger numbers, than at any time in our recorded history. This is the basis of what has come to be called 'superdiversity', an idea introduced (separately) by Steve Vertovec of Oxford University and myself almost a decade ago.[23] The term recognises that our social diversity can no longer be characterised by a simple binary division between those who are white and those who are not. Superdiversity features many differences between over a dozen significant ethnic groups. Those differences are not just racial, nor are they just a function of being new to Britain. The divisions could be described as ethnocultural – and they rest on deeply held values and behaviours, which will not lightly be abandoned by Jewish, or (multiracial) Muslim communities for example.

There are two related, but separate, sets of serious social problems associated with 21st century superdiversity. Our historical process of organic integration does not offer an answer to either.

One set of issues arises from the decline in overt bigotry. The evidence is that rather than producing integrated societies in which race and ethnicity count for less and less in our destinies, western societies are *more and more* stratified by these characteristics. Different racial, ethnic and cultural groups display *objective* differences in behaviour, achievement and outcomes, often for reasons largely unconnected to discrimination. In our brave new world, instead of social classes or castes being distinguished by Greek letters, as in Aldous Huxley's novel, they can now be differentiated by skin colour or cultural symbols.

The second set of emerging concerns swirls around the question of *offence*. Increasingly, the world-views of very different social identity groupings are colliding. Incompatible attitudes to sex, religion, belief and the rule of law are producing frictions for which the tried and trusted social lubricants seem just too thin.

So far, attempts by both right and left to deal with these flashpoints have been either incendiary or ineffective. Brisk, commonsense conservatives theatrically eschew what they call political correctness; more combative right-wing spirits look around for the nearest cultural wasps' nest so that they can poke a stick into it. But identity is not territory that the centre-right has sought to make its own until very recently. In practice, the world of identity politics has been dominated by the centre-left for the last fifty years.

3

Liberals like myself have made the running. But rather than confronting today's challenges, we have tended to prevaricate, stuck in the past. We have been far too slow to acknowledge the fact that race itself is no longer a purely black and white affair. We have been even less enthusiastic about accepting that the different sets of values and behaviours prevalent in some ethnocultural communities present a serious challenge to the process of integration in our society.

The typical response of Britain's political and media elite confronted with awkward facts has been evasion, because – we say – talking about these issues won't solve the problem; instead, it will stigmatise vulnerable minority groups. Any attempt to ask whether aspects of minority disadvantage may be self-inflicted is denounced as 'blaming the victim'. Instead, we prefer to answer any difficult questions by focusing on the historic prejudices of the dominant majority. In short, it's all about white racism.

This stance just won't do any more. In fact, in today's superdiverse society, it is dangerously misguided. Social liberals have to make a decision. Do we stand by our fundamental values at the risk of offending others; or should our desire to preserve social unity be allowed to compromise much of the social progress of the past half-century? In my view, squeamishness about addressing diversity and its discontents risks allowing our country to sleepwalk to a catastrophe that will set community against community, endorse sexist aggression, suppress freedom of expression, reverse hard-won civil liberties, and undermine the liberal democracy that has served this country so well for so long.

Worst of all it may destroy popular support for the values that have, in my opinion, characterised the greatest political advances in my lifetime: equality and solidarity. This essay makes the case for the defence of those values; and for an entirely new approach to the downsides of diversity: *active integration*.

It's not all black and white

I have always been, and remain, an advocate of both equality and diversity in modern societies. I have devoted a good part of my personal and professional energy to highlighting instances of racial and other injustice. It has been my good fortune that I have had the means, as a writer and broadcaster to bring those issues to public notice. Yet the proposition that *all* ethnocultural differences stem from majority prejudice has always made me uneasy.

First, modern science – particularly advances in 'big data' – demonstrates that different ethnic and cultural groups, even after several generations in the same geographical space, do not always come to share the same behaviours, preoccupations or capabilities. The recent histories of multiethnic societies all over the world and under very different political systems bear this out – India, Latin America, the United States, the Soviet Union, and now China all remain bedevilled by unresolved ethnocultural conflict.

But there is a second, more profoundly dispiriting implication that arises from our liberal prevarications. The premise that any kind of under-achievement or failure amongst people of colour must stem solely from unequal treatment by the dominant society implies that all those who come from minority groups have no agency other than that allowed by whites. People of colour, for example, become puppets of others' prejudices, with no capability of managing or improving their own lives. This is patronising guff, a liberal prejudice that consigns people of colour to being passive victims, without independence or initiative, only significant in public life when they are available to be saved by others. As I have written elsewhere, it is faintly sickening that black lives only seem to matter when their suffering benefits white politicians.[4]

These liberal evasions have been perpetrated by many people who should know better. But for many people of good will, it may be the only way to avoid confronting an inconvenient truth: that some minority groups hold very different values and ambitions than those commonly held amongst the dominant majority; that those values and ambitions are even further away from liberal ideals than the average; and that because they are sincerely held by those groups, they aren't going to change any time soon. The European social liberal clings to the belief that we are essentially the same 'under the skin' in the desperate hope that, with time, 'liberal' values will inevitably prevail amongst people of all backgrounds.

This leads us to a dangerous contradiction. It is hard to see how those who claim to respect the multiethnic, multiracial society under the banner of 'multiculturalism' can genuinely be embracing ethnic difference, whilst at the same time dismissing those ethnocultural groups who do not share their outlook on, say, sexual orientation, as primitives who will one day learn better and adopt the ways of Western liberals. We cannot simultaneously 'celebrate' the marvellous diversity of London's restaurant scene and at the same time blandly assert that unattractive aspects of the cultures which produce the capital's varied cuisines are merely holdovers from earlier, less enlightened generations.

Today, even liberal voices have started to express some doubts. And recent events, it seems, will not allow us to turn a blind eye for much longer.

This isn't a problem confined to any single cultural or ethnic minority. During my time as chair of the Equality and Human Rights Commission, amongst the most difficult and contentious decisions I had to take involved legal action against individuals and businesses unwilling to treat lesbian and gay couples in the same way as others. Their reasons, they claimed, arose from a deep and sincere Christianity. In several cases, the people on the other side of the case were of African or African Caribbean backgrounds. They came from countries where being gay still attracts a formal punishment of many years' imprisonment – and the informal possibility of being lynched. There was no doubt in my mind that their stance would be supported by an overwhelming majority of people who share my ethnocultural background. I had no doubt that the action I had to take would be unpopular amongst black communities.

Of course, there are similar issues arising in Jewish, Hindu and other minority communities. But the most sensitive cause of conflict in recent years has been the collision between majority norms and the behaviours of some Muslim groups.

In particular, the exposure of systematic and longstanding abuse by men, mostly of Pakistani Muslim origin in the North of England, led to months of handwringing as to whether the fact of the perpetrators' ethnicity should even be reported by the media. It took the publication of two official reports, commissioned by the local authority and by government ministers, finally to break through the wall of denial.

Elsewhere in Europe, there has, until recently, been less focus on the cultural impact of immigration. But at the start of 2016 the consequences of the continent's new diversity exploded. The risks that Europe now faces could not have been more starkly demonstrated than by the behaviour of immigrant men towards women in German cities.

Migrants against women

The German Chancellor, Angela Merkel has, since 2010, been quite clear that her country needed to be open to new immigration. Estimates based on current birth rates projected a fall in Germany's working age population of almost a third over the next 45 years.[5] She was not unaware of the dangers of unchecked and rapid immigration; the Chancellor initiated a huge integration programme of *Willkommenskultur* ('welcome culture') including, for example, 800 hours of free tuition for every new immigrant. The price tag has been so large that the Chancellery declines to put a figure on it. All that German officials will say is that the federal government will spend a total of €8 billion *this year alone* to cope with the *extra* numbers from the surge of asylum seekers in 2015.

The Germans were gambling that, with effective planning, they could absorb large numbers of migrants. In fact, over the past four decades, Germany had successfully managed the settlement of 4 million Turkish *gastarbeiter*. But as of the start of this year, it has become clear that the gamble may not have come off.

In January, shocking allegations emerged concerning mob assaults of women by Muslim men in Cologne and other cities. Most of those arrested were immigrant men, some of whom had recently arrived as asylum seekers from the Middle East. Aside from the attacks themselves, the most alarming element of these incidents was that both the German authorities and media sought to suppress news of their occurrence. When this proved impossible to sustain, they went out of their way to minimize the significance of the ethnicity of the attackers, claiming that it would be wrong to link the events with the recent wave of largely Muslim immigration to Germany by asylum seekers.

Oddly, the proponents of this view did not seem to realise that their defence suggested an even more alarming picture – that the perpetrators, who were, by common consent, of Arab and North African appearance, were people who had been in Germany for some time. If that were the case, their scandalous behaviour could not be explained away by the suggestion that they were new to European ways. Instead it would imply that a group of Germany's five million or so settled Muslim migrants had, for some reason, suddenly and inexplicably decided to run amok; and that to some Muslim men in Germany, basic norms of decent behaviour are irrelevant.

Even the local political authorities joined in the farce. The mayor of Cologne, who had herself been the victim of a knife attack by a xenophobic white German less than a year previously, tried to have it both ways. In spite of evidence to the contrary from her own police chief, she asserted that it was 'improper' to blame recent migrants; but then advised women in public to stay at least an arm's length away from possible attackers –

presumably with men of Arab or North African appearance in mind.

It has since emerged that the Germans are not alone in experiencing this kind of cultural conflict. Over a decade ago, similar problems were identified, but not widely spoken of, in the European country which has been most generous in its openness to asylum and immigration: Sweden.

In 1996, one of the Swedish government's own agencies, the National Council for Crime Prevention, said that male immigrants were 23 times more likely to commit rape than the average; these astonishing numbers could perhaps have been explained as a consequence of various factors – small numbers, new immigration, and the effects of trauma on immigrants from war zones.

But as early as 2002, a little-noticed study by academics at Karlstadt University concluded that 85 per cent of all those sentenced to more than two years' imprisonment for rape were foreign born or second generation immigrants. The number of rapes in Sweden grew dramatically – from 421 in 1975 to 5,960 in 2010;[6] and in that year more than half of those convicted were identified as immigrants. The total is still rising; in 2014 it was 6,697.

Attempts to explain these problems as the outcome of sex ratio imbalances have foundered. Similar concerns have arisen in countries and in years where no such imbalance existed – in the UK, and in Germany, Holland and Finland.

Efforts to detach these mass attacks from the men's cultural background have looked increasingly incredible. It is only five years since the CBS news correspondent Lara Logan, reporting from Cairo's

Tahrir Square, was manhandled and sexually assaulted by a crowd of men. In this respect at least, we should have heard the warning that some immigration would bring with it values and behaviour at odds with those familiar to Europeans; and we are only at the start of this story.

The demographic time-bomb

The UK has so far been somewhat complacent about its own record. There is no significant far-right or nativist party in our politics; in January 2016, the noxious British National Party quietly slipped out of existence, crippled by internal feuding and financial debt (mostly brought about, I am pleased to say, by legal action I took as chair of the Equality and Human Rights Commission).

Nonetheless, like the French, Germans and Swedes, our demography means that we will not be able to live in denial for much longer. The speed and scale of change in ethnocultural diversity are becoming impossible to ignore.

According to the Mapping Integration Project at the Policy Exchange think-tank, between 2008 and 2013, there was a 31 per cent increase in the number of ethnic minority children starting school in England. The analysis found that 61 per cent of them began their education in schools where ethnic minorities form the majority of the student body. In London, the figure was 90 per cent.[7]

By mid-century between a quarter and a third of Britain's population will be comprised of people of colour.[8] The visible minority population will rise from its current 13 per cent to between 25 and 35 per cent by 2050. Some cities – Birmingham, Leicester, for example – will be over 50 per cent non-white British. London already feels like a different country to, say, Northumbria or Kent or Norfolk.

According to the leading demographer Philip Rees of Leeds University we can expect more than half of Britain's districts to become more like London – and the other half to be very different.[9]

Even the part of our society that typically pays little attention to current affairs, was electrified in the summer of 2015 by the nightly television reports of what was happening at Europe's margins and in the Mediterranean. At the end of 2015, it was estimated by EU officials that a million refugees had crossed the Mediterranean and the Balkans into Europe. Aid agencies say they expect a further million in 2016.[10]

It's not just the numbers that count in trying to manage the integration process; it is the character of these waves of migration. Historically, Britain has embraced many immigrant groups who were very different from the population they joined – former American slaves in the early 19th century for example. But these groups balanced their social distance with an eagerness to fit in with prevailing norms. For the first time in living memory Europe has encountered a minority group which both occupies a significant social distance from the society into which it is arriving, but which also appears resistant to the traditional process of integration. A small minority is actively opposed to values and behaviours that most Europeans take for granted.

Today there are 44 million Muslims in Europe. By 2050, that number will be 71 million – some one in 10 of the continent's population.[11] According to a 2015 poll by the firm Survation for the BBC, they hold what one respected

Muslim commentator called some 'disconcerting' atttudes. A third of UK Muslims would like their children educated separately from non-Muslims. A quarter disagreed with the statement that 'acts of violence against anyone publishing images of the Prophet could never be justified'; and a quarter were sympathetic to the 'motives' of the Charlie Hebdo killers.[12]

These facts should presage a society in a turmoil of preparation for change; and a political and media elite engaged in serious debate as to how we meet this challenge to our fundamental values. Yet whilst we hear the words racism and Islamophobia often enough, there remains a deafening silence in the air about the real dilemmas that confront our society.

A noisy silence: the language of denial

We know that the unresolved tensions between different traditions and outlooks within our society are the stuff of everyday unease amongst our fellow citizens. They threaten to erupt at any time. These anxieties lie behind the stubborn kernel of support for nationalist political parties – UKIP and the SNP for example – and the unwavering salience of immigration as a touchstone issue over the past five years.

There is no shortage of public condemnation of 'racism': complaints about discriminatory behaviour, the alleged fear of backlash against Muslims after each terrorist incident, campaigns to remove symbols of colonialism, and social media campaigns against supposedly offensive language. And they are mixed in the liberal mind with more legitimate concerns about identity issues such as the persistence of, for example, female genital mutilation in minority communities.

But these are not the topics that generate public unease. Rather it is the appearance of non-English names above the shop-fronts in the high street; the odd decision to provide only halal meat in some schools; evidence of corruption in municipal politics dominated by one ethnic group or another. Such headlines, frequently misreported, but often grounded in some real change, provoke muttering in the pub, or grumbling at the school gate. They become gathering straws in a stiffening breeze of nativist, anti-immigrant sentiment. And still, our political and media elites appear not to have scented this new wind. We maintain a polite silence masked by noisily debated public fictions such as 'multiculturalism' and 'community cohesion'. Rome may not yet be in flames, but I think I can smell the smouldering whilst we hum to the music of liberal self-delusion.

A clue as to why the UK roils in this unhappy exceptionalism lies in the history of one of the few political utterances that most British people can recognise. In Enoch Powell's 1968 speech, he too summoned up echoes of Rome with his reference to Virgil's dire premonition of the River Tiber 'foaming with much blood'.[13]

This much-studied address is, simultaneously, lauded as an epic example of the use of political rhetoric – and also as a ghastly testament to the power of unbridled free speech. Either way, it effectively put an end to Powell's career as an influential leader. Everyone in British public life learnt the lesson: adopt any strategy possible to avoid saying anything about race, ethnicity (and latterly religion and belief) that is not anodyne and platitudinous.

Of course, denial comes in several disguises. No-one ever openly admits to being afraid of race as a topic.

One of the most common forms of 'virtue-signalling'[14] is to assert solidarity with oppressed minorities in some fashion; typically, when the issue of race arises, many in our elites boast that they 'do not have a racist bone' in their bodies. Others will claim kinship of a sort – being discriminated against because of their class origins, their accent or other outsider characteristics. Either way, the act of identifying with the oppressed is a way of removing any need to do much more than display empathy.

A further strategy, much favoured by politicians, is to pretend that the problems don't exist. UKIP leader Nigel Farage argued, in an interview with me before the 2015 election, that Britain no longer needs race discrimination laws, because racial prejudice had, in effect, been vanquished.[15] This claim was considered so outlandish by journalists that the UKIP leader first backtracked, claiming that he hadn't said it; and when confronted with his own image saying exactly these words, he professed that he had said it several months ago and had forgotten the interview.

Others politicians opt for misdirection or barefaced denial. The Labour leader, Jeremy Corbyn, MP for an inner London constituency for over three decades, managed to get through his entire first conference address without mentioning the words race, racism or, astonishingly, immigration, once. His shadow home secretary, Andy Burnham, did a little better. He mentioned immigration once – but only as a reason to dislike UKIP. The leader of Britain's third party, Nicola Sturgeon of the SNP, did something similar in her own major conference speech of 2015.

It was the Conservative leader, David Cameron, who had most to say about race equality, in a rare direct reference:

> Opportunity doesn't mean much to a British Muslim if he walks down the street and is abused for his faith. Opportunity doesn't mean much to a black person constantly stopped and searched by the police because of the colour of their skin.

But even the Prime Minister did not return to his February 2011 full-frontal attack on the 'doctrine of state multiculturalism'.

There are costs to this fastidiousness. If we cannot even name some of the aspects of the problems, how can we seriously hope to address them?

Silence on the questions of racial, ethnic and cultural difference carries a special price in a democracy. When it comes to public policy, unless the choices can be expressed freely, unambiguously and clearly, how can the citizen ever express an informed preference?

In Britain, we are, of course, too polite to admit that we find some topics too difficult to speak about. Instead we just make them unintelligible. For example, during a recent series of reports on the shooting of a suspected terrorist in Paris, the BBC described the Goutte d'Or district ('drop of gold'), where the incident had taken place, as 'immigration-rich'. This rather prissy designation was presumably employed to avoid acknowledging that the area was at least a third Muslim, mostly from North and West Africa. The circumlocution may have spared some feelings, but hardly contributed to journalistic clarity.

Nothing symbolises the increasing use of apparently neutral language to mask ethnocultural difference than the technical language we now use to describe dimensions of race equality.

In a well ordered society we do need to know whether there are differences in life-chances, educational performance and so forth between ethnic and cultural groups to be able to decide whether, as a society, there is cause for public policy intervention.

There are many ways to organise this kind of segmentation; the seventeen ethnic categories used by the ONS have proven to be as good a compromise as any. What might have seemed, initially, rather fussy delineations – Black Caribbean as opposed to Black African for example – have served as valuable differentiators, as we learn that children from apparently similar ethnic backgrounds perform very differently academically.

We now know that the achievements of Chinese-heritage young people are a world away from those of young Pakistani-heritage students. Previously, all four groups would have been rolled up into a single 'non-White' average. These new insights mean that educators can focus their efforts more effectively on those who really need the extra help; resources are better used, and the effect of diversity understood more completely.

On the face of it there's no reason why the still-novel system of ONS categories should be insufficient. Yet, in the past few years, fresh, more opaque differentiators have appeared; namely, BME (black and minority ethnic) and even more mysteriously BAME (black, Asian and minority ethnic). Despite the fact that these terms have little explanatory or analytical function, and indeed tend to mask vital differences between minorities, they are now routinely used by decision makers.

These designations have become part of the priestly language of race equality which carries the unfortunate effect of discouraging the average person from engaging in debate about the topic of ethnicity in case he or she uses the wrong word in the wrong place.

The ill-fated attempt by the actor Benedict Cumberbatch to encourage Hollywood to employ more black actors in lead roles stands as a warning. He was vilified for using the old-fashioned word 'coloured' in an interview on the topic. In the ensuing furore, his main point was lost to public view. As a consequence, many of our cultural and political leaders prefer to stick to the far safer ground of gender or disability politics.

But the use of these terms has a purpose for those who coin them. They are one more brick in the wall of denial. In practice, by forcing data to be expressed as purely binary, white and not-white, they imply that all ethnic difference must be a consequence of white privilege or prejudice. They rule out the possibility that differences arise from cultural background or community preference.

As a consequence, groups of people who are culturally even more dissimilar to each other than they are to whites are treated by public policy as though they are the same. And the usage perpetuates the disempowering notion that every non-white person's destiny is simply the result of their treatment by whites. It is a caricature of the past, and a travesty of the present.

Race: a unique inhibition

A reluctance to speak openly about race is all the more puzzling given that we now have no discomfort about other aspects of identity politics. The drive to increase gender diversity on British company boards has carried all before it, shaming reluctant business bosses into recruiting women to their leadership. In spite of the largely symbolic nature of the change in marriage laws, even the Church of England hierarchy finds itself in the position of having to debate homosexuality on virtually every occasion it meets. There are probably fewer than 3,000 transsexuals in the UK; at most there are fewer than 700,000 people who 'are likely to be gender incongruent to some degree'.[16] Yet there is now virtually no taboo on debate about discrimination against trans-people.

It may be that race, and to some extent religion, impose unique inhibitions on debate. Most of us have some relationship with a person of the other gender (even journalists and politicians have mothers and fathers); and most of us can imagine being gay, lesbian, or disabled. All of us hope to live long enough to become old.

But race and ethnicity lie behind an opaque curtain. There is no surgical transformation or passage of time that allows us to cross that line; even people of dual heritage are what they are, and cannot experience life as a person of another ethnicity. So for many, the risk of saying words or making gestures which, in that alien territory, might be denounced as insensitive or offensive, means that silence always looks a better option. So strong has the culture of denial become that merely stating that we might have discomfort with the topic of race can itself become a source of controversy.

In March 2015, Channel 4 transmitted a film in which I tried, as the writer and presenter, to understand how this state of affairs had come about – and to delineate its consequences.

We said something rather simple, but to many viewers it appeared to be controversial: that fear of saying anything at all on the topics of race, ethnicity and cultural difference was leaving us unable to address some of the major challenges of our time – extremism, terrorism and segregation. Silence had led public authorities of all kinds – schools, law enforcement, social services – to shy away from confronting wicked acts for fear of having to address their ethnic or cultural component. And the reluctance to confront the dark side of the diverse society had allowed terrible crimes to go unpunished for many years – the Rotherham and Rochdale child abuse scandals for example.

Things We Won't Say About Race (That Are True) should really have had an audience of about three quarters of a million, given its late evening scheduling and its subject matter. In fact it took something like three times that number. Newspaper, radio and TV coverage ran steadily over a period of 17 days.

A print essay that was published in *The Sunday Times* was reprinted the following day in our second most widely read tabloid, the Daily Mail – combined readership around 2.5 million.

Yet the programme itself was not revelatory. It did not turn up new stories or produce new data. We simply stacked up some facts about outcomes for different ethnic groups. Many of our data points were – in my opinion – innocuous. For example, data from the professional body that oversees pharmacy shows that Indian-heritage women are eight times as likely to be qualified as pharmacists as the average. Data collected from Companies House by my colleague Professor Richard Webber shows that many large UK building firms are run by people of Irish heritage.[17]

These observations caused some viewers to squirm. Many felt even more uncomfortable about data which showed that:

- Jewish people are three times as likely to be top executives in top companies and Jewish households are on average twice as wealthy as non-Jewish households;

- Over 40 per cent of pickpocketing offences in central London were committed by Romanians;

- Caribbeans were roughly three times as likely to be murdered as whites, mostly by other people of Caribbean origin.

These were facts, no more or less provocative (or inaccurate) than the latest numbers for the UK's GDP or the levels of childhood obesity.

But the film clearly touched a nerve. It questioned some fundamental tenets of the British approach to 'organic' integration and it challenged Martin Luther King's celebrated dictum that if racial prejudice declined, other social norms would change. A person would start to be judged by the content of his or her character rather than the colour of his or her skin. King's belief was that over time, as our society became more open minded and less prone to unfair discrimination, ethnic and racial differences would be revealed to be no more important than hair colour.

The problem is that in most Western societies this simply hasn't turned out to be true. In fact, if anything the receding tide of post-war racial bigotry has simply exposed the jagged rocks of persistent cultural difference. Far from entering an era of racial harmony, both Europe and North America are experiencing what might be described as a process of steady dis-integration. Particularly here in the UK, we are having to face the fact that we are failing to cope with superdiversity. Because our historic experience of 20th century immigrant integration provides a poor template for the new challenges of the 21st century.

Integration: lessons from the empire

I am the son of immigrants. My family arrived in London from the (then) colony of British Guiana two years after the arrival of the Empire Windrush at Tilbury in 1948. I was born in London three years later. But our family's circumstances were such that my parents thought it better to send me back to the country that they still called 'home'. I grew up learning some profound lessons about diversity – and its discontents.

Like most former British colonies, British Guiana has, over the past four centuries, become a melange of ethnic groups. The British empire functioned as a gigantic labour market machine, efficiently moving skilled workers to crank up new industries in one territory, farmers to fresh pastures in another, shopkeepers to new towns in a third. So, as a child and a teenager I was lucky to enjoy the privilege of living in one of the most diverse countries in the world.

The student body at my school was as diverse as you could imagine – Europeans, Asians, Arabs, Africans, Native American. My old class lists in post-independence Guyana show names like Ali, Ishmael, Persaud, Chan, Ming, Ten Pow and Singh as well as the conventional European names given to the descendants of slaves – Adams, Harris, Alleyne, Moore – and Phillips.

But as in so much of the Empire, behind the racial and religious rainbow there lay a bitter and often violent history of ethnic feuding which still disfigures that small country. One of my own classmates and friends, Donald Rodney, in later years saw his brother, the writer and academic Walter Rodney, murdered, largely for espousing the cause of non-racial politics.

Today, Guyana remains one of the poorest nations in the world, fatally stricken by its racial and ethnic divisions, struggling to realise its natural resources. So I have seen and lived first hand with both the tantalising possibilities of diversity – and the awful consequences of the absence of integration.

That childhood taught me several lessons.

First, that it is a natural instinct to stick to your own kind and to mistrust others. Much as, post-Martin Luther King, our children are taught otherwise, integration isn't an automatic human response to diversity. It's a learned behaviour; and that behaviour can be inherited – or not.

Second, that knowing more about each other is no guarantee of harmony. In Guyana – as in Northern Ireland – the longer and closer a look the different groups took at each other, the less they liked what they saw.

Third, the absence of integration isn't always just down to an absence of opportunity. It *sometimes* is; when my parents came to London some people really would move out of the street when they moved in. But that isn't always the case.

Today, East African Asian and Jewish millionaires, who can afford to buy homes in any part of the capital, choose to congregate in the perfectly pleasant but undistinguished suburbs of north-west London. Our schools are more segregated than they need to be, largely because of parental choice. Work by Miles Hewstone and his team at Oxford University shows that, whilst positive mixing does promote better community relations, it doesn't happen by chance.[18]

Finally, integration has to be a two-way street. To make diverse societies work, both majority and minority have to change. The new minority has to respect the values of the old majority; and the old have to make room for the new.

When my family arrived in Britain, none of these lessons had been learnt. The so-called integration process was far simpler then: you learned what everyone else did, and you copied it. Today we call it assimilation.

Assimilation: right question, wrong answer

I was the last of my parents' 10 children to start life as a subject of the British Empire, and the first born on British soil. Half a decade after the arrival of the Windrush the numbers of immigrants were in the tens of thousands; a tiny number compared to a population of some eight million foreigners living in Britain today.[19] Our families lived on the margins of cities only just recovering from the privations of war. We occupied miserable, rat-infested, overcrowded slums, policed by gangsters.

But like most immigrants we were just grateful to be here at all. The recent political arguments over the so-called bedroom tax would have seemed extraordinary to the Windrush generation. As the youngest child in the family, I slept in my parents' bedroom well into my seventh year. My two adult sisters and a cousin shared bunks in a room upstairs. When they left, we took in lodgers. The concept of a spare room just did not exist for us.

Our parents asked little of Britain except regular work, kept themselves to themselves, focused on fitting in and getting on. Many immigrants spent their working hours in factories, hospitals, garages and offices where the majority of their workmates were also immigrants. At weekends, they spent their time with family and friends, only occasionally rubbing shoulders with 'English' people.

As a consequence, the immigrants of the Windrush generation had little impact on the society. Most people, including the immigrants themselves, believed that it would only be a matter of time until they packed up and went home, taking their savings with them. England would have served its purpose.

There were also, relative to today, few immigrants. They spoke English, they were Christians. They taught us, their children, to believe in the beneficence of the mother country. Thinking themselves temporary guests the Windrush generation behaved with exemplary politeness, even to the extent of mimicking the manners of a society that, for the white majority, was already fading.

LP Hartley's novel *The Go-Between* appeared in 1953, the year in which I was born. Its Edwardian social landscape was still familiar to the imaginations of most Brits, if not in their details, at least in its manners. 'In those days dress was much more ceremonious and jackets were not lightly discarded,' writes his narrator. As far as I can recall, my own father, born in 1910, despite spending most of his working life in uniform – the Army, the railways and the Post Office – never left the house without a tie, never dressed for work without a stiff collar. These immigrants were never going to frighten the horses.

The path followed by the Windrush generation is no longer open to today's immigrants. Britain is changing at an extraordinary pace. The range of outlooks in our society is probably unprecedented. In a country used to stability and gradual change, the frictions being generated by our increasing diversity threaten our historic tranquility.

Successful integration, British-style, has always relied on gradual change. For the past few hundred years we managed our domestic cultural, ethnic and religious differences through a rather stately minuet, with the steps of the dance communicated through a series of nods, winks and muted gestures. Newcomers are encouraged gradually to learn and to copy the attitudes and behaviours of the society they have joined.

But during the past half-century, the number of immigrants, and their children and grandchildren has risen, first steadily, then rapidly, and now at dramatic speed, fuelled by further immigration and higher birth rates amongst young, foreign born families. We are now remaking our nation at speed. It's not a familiar experience for the UK.

Sophisticated studies by, for example, Ipsos MORI show that levels of popular anxiety are largely unrelated to numbers of immigrants, net or otherwise.[20] By and large the worries relate to the perceived speed of change in society as a whole rather than any specific personal experience.

The speed of change isn't our only problem. So is the direction. For many in Britain today, The Go-Between's famous opening sentence – 'The past is a foreign country; they do things differently there' – might just as easily be re-written about the present. They look around and see a country transformed, and while a small and largely fortunate minority embraces the change, the majority remains bewildered and uneasy. For that majority, it is the country they live in that now feels like an alien place; many don't much like what it's become.

They are even less enthusiastic about what appears to be up ahead.[21]

Britain has always treated integration as a two-way process of mutual accommodation. The settled majority shuffles, shifts and flexes to accommodate the new folk, sometimes grumpily, sometimes generously. And we even, in time, find ways to seize the traits we find attractive and make them the preserve of the whole nation (think of chicken tikka masala, Lenny Henry's galére of Caribbean caricatures and Prince Philip's robust views, to name but three cherished institutions inspired by immigrants). But it is clear that today we just don't have the time we used to enjoy, in order to achieve integration between different groups. And the majority isn't quite as ready to shift in the way it used to be.

Moreover it's becoming clear that given the social distance of some minority communities – both from other minorities and from the dominant majority – the old tools associated with organic integration are unsuited to the new demographic mix. In a superdiverse society, there is no guarantee that we can achieve the steady convergence of values between different groups that underpins successful integration. Even if there were, the signs are that this process would just take too long left to itself. We need a process of active integration.

I discuss below what this new process might constitute. But before we address the future, we will need to unwind a great deal of the past.

I have already mentioned one historic error – to construct race relations as a purely black-white problem. We made this, and other, mistakes partly because of our own history, and partly by a disastrous mimicking of the politics of a nation with a radically different racial history and configuration, the United States.

Race relations, American-style

In 1965, a new, reforming, Labour home secretary, Roy Jenkins, came to office determined to attack the racial discrimination he considered a scar on Britain's social landscape. Some of his concern was pragmatic. He, like others, could see the writing on the wall. The first generation of children of Caribbean immigrants had started to take their places in British schools. It was clear that this group was no longer planning to return to the Caribbean. They were here to stay, and the fact of their presence had to be recognised. Jenkins made clear that his aim was integration, but not in the old assimilationist sense. Integration, he said, should not be thought of as:

> ...a flattening process of assimilation, but as equal opportunity, accompanied by cultural diversity, in an atmosphere of mutual tolerance.[22]

In other words, stop discrimination, and, in the language of the time, 'let a hundred flowers bloom'. The instrument that the new Labour government chose to deliver its vision was, almost inevitably, the law. Last year marked the fiftieth anniversary of the passage of Britain's first anti-discrimination law – the Race Relations Act of 1965, the first legislation to outlaw the colour bar. This relatively mild set of prohibitions had been provoked by the existence of a colour bar in housing and jobs.

The housing problem had exploded into Britain's consciousness with the Notting Hill race riots in 1958,

largely provoked by the resentment of young white men at the arrival of Caribbean immigrants in London, competing for housing and (it was said) the attention of young women.

Tension had been growing in the area because of the post-war housing shortage. The good fortune of the new immigrants was that they had come to a country with too few workers. Windrush migrants would say that they could lose a job in the morning and find a new one in the afternoon. Their misfortune was that it was also a country with too few homes for its workers, old or new. The immigrants found themselves the objects of a colour bar, against which there was no legal protection. The infamous 'no niggers' signs were entirely lawful.

The problem wasn't just limited to petty discrimination by individual landladies. It was not until the 1970s that local authorities would make council homes available to immigrants; and mortgage companies notoriously refused to lend to blacks. Most of the early Caribbean immigrants were able to buy properties only after many years of pooling their savings in the informal system that they called 'sou-sou' or 'box'. As a consequence much of the accommodation available to the immigrants like my own parents was controlled by slum landlords and their gangster associates. The practice of packing Caribbean migrants into slums became known as Rachmanism, after the most notorious of the property barons who exploited the colour bar for their own purposes.

On the employment front, though West Indians were able to find jobs, they soon found that neither talent nor endeavour could open the doors to better paid and higher status work. In 1963, the Bristol Bus Company declared that it would not employ black drivers or conductors because, it was said, white customers feared to travel late at night with black men. A boycott of the buses, organised by a young, British-born man of mixed race, Paul Stephenson, was successful in forcing the transport bosses to reverse their decision. Stephenson's cause was taken up by Labour politicians, and when Wilson won the 1964 election, a new law on race discrimination was firmly on its agenda.

But, as frequently in politics, a single incident concerning a high-profile celebrity also shaped ministers' ideas. Twenty years before Wilson came to power, one of the most well-known black men in Britain, the cricketer Learie Constantine had been asked to leave a London hotel after one night, despite having made a booking for a longer stay. The management of the hotel company made no bones about the reasons; they were anxious about possible complaints from white American servicemen, who were used to racial segregation, legally enforced in their own country.

Constantine, already sensitive, like most West Indians of his generation, to slights because of his colour, sued the company and won. For the following 20 years, he became an advocate for racial equality; it is thought that he lost his position as Trinidad's High Commissioner to the UK because of his public and un-diplomatic support for the Bristol bus boycott. Constantine, a lawyer, and later to become the first of the Caribbean wave to be appointed to the House of Lords, added his voice to those lobbying the new Labour government for a new anti-discrimination law.

The appeals fell on receptive ears. Jenkins was advised by Anthony Lester, a young lawyer, later to become one the UK's principal human rights advocates. Lester had spent some time in the US observing the emergence of the civil rights movement. Lester's experience convinced him that most of the issues of race relations could be traced to straightforward colour prejudice. And like most liberals, he strongly believed in the message preached by Dr Martin Luther King that the reason such prejudice was unjust was that we were, in fact, pretty much the same under the skin. In effect, race and ethnic differentials were to be treated largely as a function of majority prejudice.

The new Labour government took as its template the new civil rights legislation of the USA. The problem was that the American legislation had been drafted to tackle a very different history – the legal legacy of slavery and Jim Crow laws. Our 'race' problem was quite different – one of a lack of social integration, based on our colonial history, rather than one of legal prohibitions arising from needs of the plantation system.

An astute American from the South once explained it to me in the following way. In the British Empire, whites always lived and socialised very separately from 'natives'; there was no need for legislation to keep their lives separate, as they occupied wholly different worlds. In the USA, on the other hand, where slaveholdings tended to be quite small – tens rather than hundreds of slaves – whites and blacks lived cheek by jowl, and the legal prohibitions were necessary to ensure that white privilege and property was properly protected (even from the masters' own mixed-race progeny).

I think this neat differentiation helps to explain why American solutions still seem inadequate to our situation. And even in the United States today, as it becomes more ethnically fragmented, it is becoming clear that a multiethnic society needs more than legislation to tackle the frictions of superdiversity.

Asian-Americans, for example, would say that their advance is just as likely to be frustrated by the application of affirmative action in favour of, say, African-Americans as it is by white prejudice.

In the past 20 years, the British reliance on the law to tackle ethnic and cultural relations has exposed further shortcomings in our approach. Since the mid-1990s, the scope of anti-discrimination law has steadily widened, with cross-party support. Discrimination law was amended to encompass disability in 1995. Since 2010 six further grounds, including sexual orientation, as well as religion and belief have been added. But an even more significant change was the decision to create duties on legal authorities to promote equality of various kinds – the so-called positive duties. Those, like me, who supported the introduction of these positive duties saw them as a way of preventing discrimination before it took place. In theory, requiring institutions to pay due regard to their policies and practices made sense. But things haven't turned out that way, and what looked like a brilliant legal innovation may have paved the way into a bureaucratic and political quagmire.

The Macpherson Inquiry problem

The concept of the positive duty arose from the long-running failure of the authorities to respond to the death of the black teenager Stephen Lawrence in 1993. The official inquiry into the murder, chaired by Sir William Macpherson, charted in painstaking detail the failure of the Metropolitan police to investigate the killing, as well as the atrocious treatment of the Lawrence family. The inquiry then set out its analysis of the causes of the failure. It used the phrase 'institutional racism' to describe what it had found. This was a mistake whose consequences are still felt today.

The idea behind institutional racism was originally put forward in 1967 by the radical Trinidadian-American activist Stokely Carmichael.[23] He and his co-author, Charles Hamilton, later defined it as persistent racial bias which stemmed from 'the operation of established and respected forces in the society'. The important point was that Carmichael and Hamilton were referring, not to individual people, but to abstract 'forces', organisations and institutions. Their analysis was in large part a critique of the Martin Luther King philosophy. They thought that King's emphasis on transforming the position of America's Negroes (as he would have called them) through changing individual whites' attitudes was simply naive.

Carmichael and Hamilton believed that even if they could persuade whites voluntarily to abandon their privilege (they were pretty sceptical that this could ever happen) it wouldn't necessarily make any practical difference. They argued that even in places where people of all races were committed to equality and there was no intention to discriminate, institutional culture and inertia could still result in the persistence of racial disadvantage. They took as their examples the universities, churches and the civil rights movement itself. Indeed, they claimed that the biases were often so subtle, no-one could detect a pattern of discrimination at all.

This was, and is, a perfectly respectable proposition. It is to some extent supported by modern research using 'big data' analytics, based on the study of millions of transactions in, for example, financial services or the retail sector. But none of these data were available to

Carmichael and Hamilton in 1967. Their case was largely theoretical. They insisted that a history of legally enforced discrimination had inscribed patterns of racial inequality in American life that could not be changed without equally thoroughgoing legal remedies, such as affirmative action.

Not much of this historical detail figured in the Macpherson Inquiry's report. Its reception was mixed. The government, which had commissioned it, welcomed it. But the police – and much of the media – absent the history of the phrase 'institutional racism' - took the recommendation as a charge that all the individuals who worked for the accused institutions themselves stood guilty of racism as individuals. In a sense, the proposition was that people would commit discrimnatory acts unless they were policed and prevented by the state.

Accordingly, the new Labour administration pressed ahead with amendments to the race relations legislation in line with the spirit and letter of the inquiry recommendations. New laws required all public bodies to demonstrate that their policies and practices were free of the potential for discrimination. It was considered important enough for the government to make an extra £3 million per annum available to the Commission for Racial Equality on top of its £16 million government grant in order to monitor and enforce the new duties.

There's no direct evidence that the new law has had much impact on race discrimination. But it did have three other effects. First, it alerted some public bodies, which had no written policy about race equality, to the fact that they needed one, and provoked a flurry of consultation and document writing, without much action. Second, it triggered the creation of a substantial bureaucratic machine – developing and issuing guidance, for example – to try to give the new laws teeth.

But most worryingly the Macpherson fallout introduced a new concept to Britain: when it came to race discrimination, those who worked for public bodies were probably guilty unless and until they could be shown to be innocent. It also paved the way for a new piece of European jurisprudence, which, to date, has provoked astonishingly little comment.

In the late 1990s, the European Commission and the Council of Europe both began to issue streams of guidance on legal remedies to discrimination of various kinds. In 2006 the parent body of the European Court of Justice, the Council of Europe, issued new rules which, in essence, instructed the court to reverse the burden of proof in discrimination cases:

> ...when persons who consider themselves wronged because the principle of equal treatment has not been applied to them establish, before a court or other competent authority, facts from which it may be presumed that there has been direct or indirect discrimination, it shall be for the respondent to prove that there has been no breach of the principle of equal treatment... If the respondent is unable to explain the treatment using objective reasons unrelated to discrimination, he will be liable for a breach of non-discrimination law.[24]

In short, once an allegation of discrimination had been credibly established, it became the employer's responsibility to show that he or she was not guilty. The problem is that if such a provision has ever been appropriate for the UK it now threatens to become more of a problem than a solution.

Guilty until proven innocent

This novel step, as radical as it might seem, aside from undermining basic civil liberties simply does not respond adequately to the challenge of a superdiverse society. The legal remedy of placing the burden of proof on the alleged racist seems inappropriate in 2016. There are three principal reasons.

First, we know that racial disadvantage owes less and less to individual attitudes. As a people the British are simply more tolerant and less prejudiced than when race relations legislation was first proposed. That does not mean that the spirit of Bernard Manning has died; but it is retired and hopefully breathing its last. We are just less likely to face overt and deliberate acts of individual bigotry.

Twenty years ago, when asked by the British Social Attitudes Survey, a representative sample of British people, how they would feel about having, for example, a female boss, gay neighbours, or a black or Asian in-law, more than a quarter of survey respondents would express some unease – usually by saying that they had no worries personally but that they thought there might be colleagues, neighbours or other relatives who were not so open-minded. Today, researchers struggle to find one in 10 people admitting to these attitudes. And amongst people under thirty the very questions used in the 1980s would seem incomprehensible.

Second, the premise of the positive duties is that disadvantage results mostly from unequal treatment. But increasingly we can now trace many differences to choice, not just by individuals but collective preferences by ethnic and cultural groups. This is both more prevalent and less hidden than in the past. We now understand that each of us is a composite of many things – our family history, our professions, gender, race and so on. As our societies have become more affluent and more secure we want to live lives that are more openly in tune with all aspects of our identities – we want everyone to know who and what we are. We want to bring our whole selves to work. Hence gay pride, disability rights, and the black is beautiful movement.

In essence, well-off societies are enjoying more freedoms, and people are more relaxed about being seen to conform to their own inherited and community behaviours. This means that, for example, the children of Hindu heritage Britons are three times as likely to grow up in homes where parents are married, compared to children of African-Caribbean origin. According to the 2011 census, Jamaican children were four times as likely as Indian children to be living in lone parent households.[25] The collective cultural preferences of each group leads to life-chances which are very different for each community.

Third, because of technical advances in data gathering and monitoring, we now know a great deal more about the systemic effect of belonging to an ethnocultural identity group than we used to. The advent of big data is about to transform both our understanding and our approach to race equality.

Diversity and big data

In practice, the perfectly integrated society is one in which an individual's life chances, preferences, and behaviours are randomly related to his or her race or religion. A sociologist would probably call it a society in which race carries no explanatory power in predicting outcomes. Some would say that religious background should be regarded similarly. Parliament agrees, having added religion and belief to the range of characteristics which are thought to be causes for protection against discrimination.

A journalist might translate this as meaning that when I walk into the room, my skin colour or shape of features should give you no clue as to whether I would be a dustman, a doctor or a bus driver. Yet, in spite of serious efforts to achieve this happy outcome, we are, in many ways, almost as far from that ideal today as we were when my parents arrived. Some minority groups remain unsuccessful in education and employment three generations on.

For some groups, just being able to see the glass ceiling beloved of gender politics would be a fine thing. They are, in fact, trapped in the ethnic cellar, with no prospect of the door opening even to the ground floor. This raises a difficult question to which we, unfortunately, do not know the answer. As ethnic groups try to climb out of the cellar, how much of their failure is caused by the door repeatedly being closed in their faces; and how much is due to the fact that they are handcuffed to heavy cultural baggage that they really could leave at the foot of the stairs?

Big data should help us to understand the ratio between the two. We know that some differences and some disadvantages are inherent and generally speaking inextricably associated with our race, gender and so forth.

Some differences are harder to explain:

- West Indians and people from the Western Isles share a passion: condensed milk;
- The UK's biggest donors to human rights charities are Swedes and Jews...
- ...but Africans give more often – especially if you ask them in person;
- The new owner of the local petrol station is probably going to be a Sri Lankan Tamil;
- Chinese families respect old people, but prefer to live in new houses.

More recently, we have shown that the most commonplace of leisure activities – viewing of terrestrial TV channels – is sharply coded by ethnicity. In 2015, the top twenty most popular programmes amongst all viewers shared just ten titles with the top twenty amongst minority viewers. Well-known titles such as Downton Abbey, Broadchurch, Call the Midwife, and Poldark – hold little appeal for non-white viewers.[26]

Big data doesn't explain these preferences. But it does help us understand that neither are our differences just due to unequal treatment, nor are they just a cage we're forced into from birth.

Does it matter? Yes it does. In the TV industry, the expression 'water-cooler television' refers to a programme or event that everyone sees and talks about. It reminds us that this, the nation's most common leisure pastime is also a vital part of society's connective tissue. If some groups of people are cut off from that connective tissue; if they can't be part of the water-cooler conversation, what may just appear to

Table 1: Most Popular Programmes: All vs People of Colour

TOP 20 RATING TV PROGRAMMES

ALL INDIVIDUALS

	Channel	Programme Title	000s
1	BBC 1	THE GREAT BRITISH BAKE OFF	15,055
2	ITV	BRITAIN'S GOT TALENT (SERIES 9)	12,746
3	BBC 1	STRICTLY COME DANCING: THE RESULTS	12,469
4	BBC 1	EASTENDERS	11,571
5	BBC 1	NEW YEAR'S EVE FIREWORKS	11,479
6	ITV	I'M A CELEBRITY – GET ME OUT OF HERE!	11,329
7	ITV	DOWNTON ABBEY (SERIES 6)	10,924
8	ITV	BROADCHURCH	10,861
9	BBC 1	CALL THE MIDWIFE	10,729
10	BBC 1	THE VOICE UK	10,099
11	BBC 1	DOCTOR FOSTER	10,094
12	ITV	CORONATION STREET	10,082
13	ITV	THE X FACTOR (SERIES 12)	9,764
14	ITV	RUGBY WORLD CUP 2015 ENG V WAL	9,744
15	BBC 1	MRS BROWN'S BOYS	9,512
16	BBC 1	MIRANDA	9,509
17	BBC 1	STICK MAN	9,277
18	BBC 1	DEATH IN PARADISE	9,103
19	BBC 1	POLDARK	8,746
20	BBC 1	AND THEN THERE WERE NONE	8,611

BLACK, ASIAN AND MINORITY ETHNIC

	Channel	Programme Title	000s
1	BBC 1	NEW YEAR'S EVE FIREWORKS	1,453
2	BBC 1	EASTENDERS	1,213
3	BBC 1	THE GREAT BRITISH BAKE OFF	1,173
4	ITV	THE X FACTOR RESULTS (SERIES 12)	1,130
5	BBC 1	THE APPRENTICE	1,110
6	ITV	BRITAIN'S GOT TALENT (SERIES 9)	1,057
7	BBC 1	THE VOICE UK	886
8	BBC 1	THE FA CUP FINAL: ARSENAL V ASTON VIL	785
9	BBC 1	STICK MAN	761
10	BBC 1	STRICTLY COME DANCING	753
11	BBC 1	WIMBLEDON MEN'S FINAL	737
12	BBC 1	FILM: BRAVE (2012)	727
13	BBC 1	CITIZEN KHAN	722
14	BBC 1	BRYAN ADAMS ROCKS BIG BEN LIVE	698
15	ITV	GENERAL ELECTION LEADERS' DEBATE	669
16	ITV	I'M A CELEBRITY – GET ME OUT OF HERE!	663
17	BBC 1	DOCTOR WHO	660
18	BBC 1	THE QUEEN'S CHRISTMAS MESSAGE	641
19	ITV	CORONATION STREET	635
20	BBC 1	THE GREAT COMIC RELIEF BAKE OFF	623

Sources: BARB (left) Webber Phillips (right)

Note: Programmes are highlighted if they appear in both top 20 lists.

be a private preference can quickly become a kind of social apartheid.

Other kinds of difference are more obviously significant; not least those which concern our health, safety or education – all crucial indicators of our life- chances.

We really aren't the same under the skin

The question of whether there are intrinsic differences between ethnocultural groups is one that most public figures would prefer to avoid. However, the power of modern information technology is daily making it clear that, even if we cannot understand some differences, we cannot ignore them. Nor will these differences disappear. They are not simply symptoms of unequal treatment.

Let's start with what, to some, will seem a trivial example. When the men lined up for the 100 metres at last year's World Athletics Championships few were sure who was going to win – Usain Bolt or Justin Gatlin.

But what was remarkable was that all but one of the men alongside them was black, descendants of West Africans; and all but two were from families who had once been slaves. Exactly the same held true in the women's final. Analysis of historic records shows that something similar has featured in every Olympic sprint final since Jesse Owens won four gold medals in the 1936 Berlin Olympics.

The data do not allow us to hypothesise the reason that this pattern exists. But it does present us with a paradox; and the principles involved aren't unique to race or ethnicity. We organize competitive categories, ostensibly in a 'common sense way'; but actually, our 'common sense' is entirely based on our understanding of the probabilities. We do not allow men and women to compete in most sport. That is not because no woman will ever beat any man in an athletic contest, but because the *probabilities* at elite level tell us that it's so unlikely as to make unisex competition almost meaningless and clearly unfair.

In Paralympic sports, this principle has been developed to an extraordinary degree of detail. The Paralympic authorities have worked hard to create an immensely intricate system of classification to ensure that people with different types of impairment are treated fairly when in competition. In the men's 100m sprint alone, there are 15 different categories of impairment, each of which only permits competitors with a specific disability to particpate. This does not imply that any group of athletes is more or less valued than athletes in a separate category. They are merely different.

But most people's 'common sense' would lead them to consider categorising athletes according to skin colour or racial background as an absurd, insulting process. But here the obstacle to the rational categorisation exists for reasons of history, rather than for reasons of fairness. Is it, for example, really fair that the descendant of West African slaves like Usain Bolt compete against the descendants of Northern Europeans who, whatever else they are good at, are unlikely to produce a world sprint champion?

This question might be regarded as frivolous, though we know that in modern sports the stakes are extraordinarily high. Apart from national prestige, stars like Usain Bolt become extremely wealthy. Bolt himself is worth over US$20 million already and is contracted to pick up a cheque for over $4 million each year for the next decade from one sponsor alone.

Fairness amongst elite athletes may seem intriguing, but largely irrelevant to everyday life. Yet the significance of these intrinsic differences is becoming increasingly clear in the arena of public services, where the state endeavours to provide the same level of service for everyone – but is stymied by the task of providing similar satisfaction to groups who have very different expectations.

For example, the Ipsos MORI study of GP patient opinion – a sample of over 100,000 individuals – for 2013 shows that British Bangladeshi and Pakistani Muslim groups, corrected for class and geography, are 40 per cent less likely to rate their GPs as 'very good' than the average person. Yet NHS doctors are far from being an all white, all Christian grouping, prone to discriminate against people of colour. So what is it about the way that these millions of British people interact with a universal service that gives them less satisfaction?

We can't yet answer that question. But we can take some clues from a study conducted some years ago for Tower Hamlets Health Trust. And they tell us that it may have very little to do with racial discrimination, nor to do with new immigration, and everything to do with persistent differences in cultural expectations. Between 2002 and 2004 use of A&E in Tower Hamlets doubled; local hospitals struggled to meet the government's four-hour waiting target. Analysis of 200,000 attendance records, using technology developed by my colleague Richard Webber, showed that users were disproportionately Bangladeshi.

The first assumption was that this was an immigrant problem – older people who didn't really understand the system. But analysis showed that the over-users were a group with age spikes at 0-5 and 20–29 – in fact, young families with British-born parents.

Further focus groups showed that, when Mohammed or Asma fell off the slide, unlike their classmates, the decision to take children to A&E was a *family* decision. And older Bangladeshis believed that GPs were less professional – not real doctors – no white coats, no battery of intrusive tests. Targeted educational campaigns reduced the over-use in target hospitals within a year: there was a 6.4 per cent total decline in 2005/06 compared to increases of 3.6 per cent and 2.6 per cent in neighbouring hospitals. GP attendance figures rose and savings were significant at between £55-100 per visit to A&E; and the four-hour waiting targets were met.[27]

This problem was solved through marketing and campaigning rather than the use of anti-discrimination law. There are other examples emerging from other sectors of public life. Take the issue of diversity in the police for example. Avon and Somerset Police, worried about the poor scores of minority candidates in one of their online recruitment tests asked the Behavioural Insight Unit – the so-called 'nudge' unit – to help them understand what was going on.

The researchers came up with a simple plan. They adjusted the tone of a reminder email that went to all candidates, making it friendlier.

Astonishingly, this no-cost intervention had the effect of increasing the pass rate amongst ethnic minorities by 50 per cent – and in fact eliminated the gap in pass rates between whites and non-whites.[28]

The essential point is that we are now learning that problems we thought could be solved by legal or regulatory means may be better addressed by other means. Ultimately, the puzzle here is how we change human behaviour without state or legal compulsion. For advocates of equality of opportunity no arena matters more than education.

Superdiversity in schools

It is widely accepted that education, especially in the early years, can make an enormous difference to any individual's life chances. It is also now well established that different ethnocultural groups fare very differently at virtually every stage of their school career.

In the UK overall standards of achievement at 16 – GCSE level – are rising. Girls generally do better than boys. Ethnic groups vary in their average levels of achievement; but they can improve – for example African Caribbean boys, who used to trail the pack, are catching up to the rest.

However, even as change takes place, the data confronts us with one extremely consistent finding, which is echoed internationally. In most ethnic groups there is a greater than 25 per cent gap between the performance of students from poor households and the average. There is one exception: children of Chinese heritage, where the poor/not-poor gap in the UK is just two per cent – and where it doesn't really matter anyway, because poor Chinese children, over 80 per cent of whom get five good GCSEs are at least 17.5 per cent ahead of every other demographic irrespective of class.[29]

The hard question here is: what do people of Chinese heritage have that the rest of us don't? And if we can copy it, should we? Or should we regard it as a kind of inequality about which we can and should do nothing – like being able to run faster than other races? To date, there have been no official studies asking any of these questions, from government, the educational establishment or even my own former employer, the Equality and Human Rights Commission (EHRC).

Then there is the effect of ethnicity on school choice. Today parents have more opportunity to select which institution their children attend than they used to. That's a good thing. But work from Bristol University has shown that over the past 10 years parents' preference for schools with more children who are similar to their own in various ways means that most schools are more ethnically segregated than the communities in which they sit.[30]

These parents are not bigots; this is not white flight. Indeed the skewing of choice applies to those in the minority as much as it does to the dominant majority. But it does mean that our schools are changing in character. In some cities, most minority children sit in classes where there are hardly any children who do not share their ethnicity. Experience from the USA where laws have been in place for half a century to deter segregation shows that their schools have experienced the same phenomenon. American schools are now more segregated than 50 years ago when the Supreme Court ruled segregation in education unconstitutional.

Ultimately, we cannot and should not restrict choice. So how do we encourage a shared future? The surperdiverse society increasingly presents us with these difficult dilemmas, for which we will need both new tools and new ideas. In fact some of these dilemmas are already emerging, in areas of life such as education, health and the workplace. Do immigrants improve school performance? Are you more likely to recover from an illness faster if your doctor is the same race or religion as you are? Are diverse organisations more productive if teams share an ethnic or cultural background? The answer to each of these questions, one way or another could make differences of billions of pounds to our national economy. Yet what is striking about these crucial questions is that there has been so little public debate about them.

(Super) diversity and its dilemmas

It is a commonplace that ethnicity is now probably the surest and simplest predictor of educational attainment, both in Europe and North America. This insight is probably most concretely realised in the transformation of London's schools from, as it were, bottom of the class to standout success over the past 15 years.[31]

Many explanations have been advanced, including the effect of regional imbalances, but the most convincing answer has been, to my mind, the most obvious. It's demographics, stupid. Compared to 2001, there are now many more pupils from high-performing ethnic groups – Indians, Chinese, African and Polish and relatively fewer from low-achieving groups – African-Caribbeans and of course whites.

Simon Burgess, Bristol University's Professor of Economics has shown convincingly that even after accounting for family background and other factors, the improvement can be accounted for almost completely by the change in the composition of the student population.[32] Not only do the demographics favour higher performing groups; it appears that the presence of a critical mass of the high-achieving minorities lifts the performance of the children from the dominant white majority too. This helps to explain why minority-rich London and Birmingham outperform other regions.

The wise parent in London or the Midlands will therefore look hard at the ethnic composition of schools on offer – and opt for the institution with the greatest proportion of children from South and East Asian backgrounds. This might benefit some children, but increasingly would have a wider social effect. It would produce, as in the USA, a school landscape that is increasingly colour-coded – the more South Asian and Chinese heritage pupils, the higher the average level of attainment.

An overly rational society might try to deal with this disparate effect by some kind of quota system, with every school required to have a minimum number of Indian children and a maximum number of African Caribbeans for example; but given the history of exclusion in British schools, would such an approach be palatable to British tastes?

In medicine, research in the United States[33] has explored the sensitive topic of racial and ethnic concordance – in plain terms race-matching doctors and patients. Broadly speaking, most of the research suggests that concordance has little impact on health outcomes, though this is still a hotly-contested question. However, recent work does suggest something new and important: that concordance may lead to greater compliance with prescribed regimes.[34] Patients trust doctors of their own background more, are more attentive and more inclined to follow the advice given. If the doctor who gives you antibiotics is the same race as you are, you are a bit more likely to complete the course.

The Centre for Disease Control in the USA estimates that misuse of antibiotics costs between 28 and 38 billion dollars each year, as well as several thousand lives. Most of the cost is due to poor prescription or overuse, but at least part of the cost is incomplete usage by patients. Even a small dent in that bill would make a huge difference. So if we knew that assigning patients preferentially to doctors who share their ethnicity would save lives and free up resources for health care, would we agree to insert an algorithm in the booking programme for every GP surgery that matched patient and care giver?

It is in the workplace that the issues of superdiversity are likely to throw up the biggest and most explosive questions. The EHRC published an inquiry into the food processing industry in 2010, which I had commissioned in 2008. The industry employs some 400,000 people[35] of which a large proportion are immigrant workers, increasingly from Eastern Europe and Africa.

It became clear during the investigation that some companies were actively managing this new diversity amongst their staff – but not quite in the way that the Commission would recommend. In effect managers were segregating their workers by function and by shift. Many employers were quite open about their reasons, telling the investigators that:

- managers preferred particular nationalities for certain shifts as they regarded these workers as 'more reliable' or 'hardworking'

- some firms attempted to manage communication challenges or to avoid tensions by segregating shifts so that all workers spoke the same language, and

- some supervisors refused to have certain nationalities working for them on grounds of race or colour.

Aside from the straightforward bigotry in the final bullet point above, the case can be made that these arrangements were straightforward management techniques to improve productivity and communication in the workplace.

But, clearly, if the workplace is to remain a primary site of social integration such an approach to superdiversity spells disaster for our society.

These are all everyday, practical dilemmas thrown up by the advent of superdiversity. They have a real impact on our lives, our businesses and our public services. However, the last and most socially destructive challenge is an old one, appearing in a fresh guise in the digital era: what is socially acceptable speech in a superdiverse society? Who can reasonably say what to whom?

The rise and rise of hate speech

At a recent conference of Muslim scholars, I had the privilege of addressing a hundred or so people at a leading British university. Most of the audience were Muslims themselves. The event took place just a few days before Remembrance Sunday. I noted that just three people in the room displayed a poppy, myself, a (white) journalist and one Muslim attendee. Raising the point, I could see the incomprehension on the faces of those without poppies; they weren't meaning to offend, but as a group, they couldn't see why they should wear what – I imagine – they think of as a symbol of war.

The same day, I visited an industrial site – where many immigrants, mostly African and Eastern Europeans, were working. Poppies were everywhere. The norms in these two places were wholly different.

One group had clearly adapted to the mainstream; the other had not.

Many people would be offended by the fact of this disparity; others would be offended by my drawing attention to it at all. If so, we had all better get used to being furious. In recent years, the frequency with which individuals declare themselves mortally offended by someone else's words or actions have expanded. So have the grounds, sometimes to the level of the absurd: a student demonstrator arrested in 2005, for calling a police horse 'gay' is perhaps the iconic example.

Slightly more disturbing, but equally absurd, have been efforts to remove symbols of past colonialism – the statue of Cecil Rhodes at Oriel College, Oxford is a standout example; the shutting down by demonstrators of theatrical performances such as the play *Bezhti*, because of its perceived insensitivity towards Sikhs; and the disruption of performance artworks like *Exhibit B* in London, for its evocation of colonial racism.

However, the most dangerous trend in my view, has been the recent over-use of the epithet 'racist'. This word (and its close cousin, 'Islamophobe') is now freely applied to almost anyone who disagrees with liberal orthodoxy on matters of racial and religious difference. A word with such toxic associations should really be reserved for individuals or organisations which are truly malevolent and racially exclusive. It should not be devalued by simply being applied to political opponents. But it is easy to slip into this mindset.

A party such as the British National Party, which constitutionally barred people of colour from its membership, could correctly be described as 'racist'. Yet UKIP, which does not, is frequently described as racist by its opponents. However much we think its policies may lead to racial disadvantage, or whatever we suspect its members' motives to be, surely it is not the same kettle of fish as the BNP?

The widening of the use of the word 'racist' has now spread beyond political knockabout to encompass the concept of 'microaggression', borrowed from American university campuses. The idea here is that small gestures or remarks, often unintentionally, may be felt as assaults on the dignity or 'safety' of minority students. An example might be the touching of a black person's hair; not a harmful thing, but probably discourteous and certainly invasive enough to cause offence.

However, the reason that the effect of microaggresions has been turbocharged in recent months is the creeping legalisation of responses to such events. Instead of a discussion about courtesy and good manners, these microaggressions have been turned into full-scale statutory offences, triggering, as in the case of the 'Rhodes Must Fall' campaign at Oxford University, an official inquiry.

In this case, no-one has been touched, insulted or menaced. The cause of action is that a small minority of students claim to be unable to put up with the pain of having to confront the statue of the old imperialist which forms part of the façade of Oriel College. It might be argued that the best answer to their pain is the strategic distribution of blindfolds by the college, to be used by those of a sensitive disposition; or perhaps the creation of a smartphone app that plots an anti-colonialist pathway around the city, much as a cyclist can call up a map of bicycle lanes that would avoid major roads.

But Oriel College, having already moved a plaque dedicated to Rhodes, the most generous benefactor in its history, launched an official consultation into the issue. Whilst it did not, in the end, cave into the demands to shroud the statue, it has devoted more political energy to this issue than to the far more important question of why there are so few black students at the university. The explanation for this course of action is that universities, rather than being places of open debate and robust contention between alternative views, have to become 'safe spaces'. The argument is pernicious.

To understand fully how we arrived at this point would require a major study. But at least some part of this new phenomenon in the UK can be traced back to the Macpherson imbroglio. Aside from creating the idea that minorities must be assumed to have suffered discrimination and offence unless the majority can prove otherwise, the inquiry introduced another novel concept to answer the question 'what constitutes a racist incident?' In Macpherson's eyes, the definition is 'any incident which is perceived to be racist by the victim or any other person'. In other words, anyone can call any act racist, even if they themselves are unaffected, and even if the act is not thought to be racist by its object.

This definition has now been adopted by most authorities and has become the norm for public bodies. It is being applied in arenas other than race, most notably gender and transgender politics. Inevitably, this has meant that a wider and wider set of actions are now thought to be 'offensive' and thus subject to potential censorship.

Few would object to the notion that gratuitous insult is not to be encouraged; but should freedom of expression be curtailed in this way? Emphatically, no. I agree with most of the well-rehearsed reasons for rejecting the spread of this kind of 'safety'.

However, I would add one more: any limitation of free speech is, in the end, an erosion of the last defence available to minorities in a diverse society. The moment that it becomes acceptable to outlaw some kinds of words and gestures, the histories of Nazi Germany, the Soviet Union, Mao's China, for example, all show that the next step is for the majority to use the power of the state to silence all minority opinions. This is the terrible error that all those who support this new definition of 'safety' are marching us towards.

It is time to call a halt.

What now?

It is not the principal purpose of this essay to set out new solutions to the problems I have described, but to create a debate that will refine this analysis, and to provoke new ideas as to how we meet the challenge ahead. But it would be disingenuous of me not to sketch out my own prejudices as to the path we must take into the future.

The theory of 'organic' integration has clearly proved unequal to today's challenges. Oddly enough, this laissez-faire approach to nation-building and renewal has been most ardently supported by the left in politics. But even those of us on the progressive wing of politics must now surely accept that in the conditions of today's society, our reflex defence of traditional behaviours and separate communities is actually undermining one of the most cherished of left-wing values – social solidarity. This is the case made powerfully in David Goodhart's book, *The British Dream*.[36] I agree with Goodhart's basic thesis, and would take it further.

The greatest losers from the loss of social solidarity will, in the end, be minorities, whose capacity to maintain even the traditions which do not challenge mainstream values would wither in a backlash against superdiversity.

It is time for us to abandon the old idea of organic integration. We have neither the time nor, in the modern jargon, the bandwidth, to allow a natural convergence of so many different cultures and traditions. Nor, in a globalised world, with the aggressive proselytising of Islamist militancy, can we rely on the notion that every community will, with time, come to see the advantages and attractiveness of western values and ways of living.

Integration is, if anything, more important and more urgent than ever before. That is why we need a new approach, which I have called *active integration*.

This is not the old assimilationist idea in new clothing. At the heart of the process of integration remains the notion that it is a two-way street. But the problem with our rather feeble efforts over the past 30 years is that so far, most of the traffic has been in one direction – support for greater equality amongst disadvantaged groups, and pressure for open-mindedness amongst the majority. Both of these drives have to some extent been successful, though there is some way to go.

However, the traffic in the other direction has been slow and thin. Expectations of non-dominant minority groups are low, and by and large they are imposed on individuals rather than on groups. We expect new immigrants to study for citizenship tests, and to have some command of the English language. We do little to create incentives for those who do not choose to be citizens to do more than the minimum to cope with living on British soil. In some ethnic groups, the majority of women, for example, remain 'economically inactive', code for staying at home, cocooned in neigbourhoods where no-one needs to speak English or meet anyone outside their own group.

We cannot, in a free society, compel people to do things they find alien or unacceptable. I do not, for example, support the French prohibition of the niqab; how a woman dresses should be a matter for her, not for the state. However, to extend the traffic metaphor for integration, on our two-way street, whilst we do not tell drivers how to drive, when to accelerate and when to brake, we can create an environment in which their actions are constrained and their behaviour is conducive to good traffic flow. So, for example, we have speed limits; we use warning signs to reinforce the highway code. An active integration process needs a similar framework and set of signals.

So, what would an active integration regime look like?

Active integration

First, there would be new signals to institutions. I would not propose the removal of the positive equality duties on public bodies, cumbersome and bureaucratic as they are. However, I would balance those with a further duty to promote integration.

This would require organisations to show that all their actions promoted a convergence of behaviour amongst staff and suppliers. It would, for example, mean that there would be an end to production teams in factories constructed by nationality. It would make clear that the preferred and standard working language would be English. It would also require employers to keep records, not just of how many employees of different backgrounds are on the payroll, but of policies that encourage shared social activity.

The duty to integrate should be applied with some force to educational institutions. Much attention has been paid to a tiny number of Muslim and Sikh schools. This is wrong and disproportionate. Policy should really focus on the places where almost all children are educated: state schools. A duty to integrate would require schools to demonstrate that they are making efforts to give their pupils a real experience of living in a diverse society – a requirement that should apply as much to minority faith schools as it might to an exclusive public school. In practice it should spell an end to the kind of ethnic takeover of state schools seen in Birmingham during the 'Trojan Horse' scandal.

The duty should apply to charities as well as public bodies. This would mean that places of worship, both majority and minority, might be required to show the Charity Commission that they are making real efforts to open their doors to believers and non-believers. It would, for example, challenge the practice being urged on Sikh gurdwaras to prohibit the marriage of Sikhs to non-Sikhs.

Second, how should such a duty be supported and enforced? Lightly. In practice, the most effective pressure for a regime of active integration must surely be transparency. A new duty should require not just publication of data about policy, or about employment equality, but also performance on integration measures. For example, local authorities should publish annual measures of residential segregation. Segregation might become a formal consideration in decisions about establishing new residential and commercial developments. Each school should also publish information about its ethnic and cultural composition.

None of this should be subject to any enforcement regime other than that provided by the market –

householders, developers and businesses should be encouraged to consult such data in making their choices, and local authorities should make the information easily available. It may be argued that this will simply provide the basis for more segregation in communities; but in truth, most people already acquire such information informally, and use it to make their decisions. Quite often, what they think they know is out of date, or plain wrong. Making reliable data publicly available would, in fact, contribute to a lessening of prejudice.

As explained above, the provision of factual data about which children are most likely to succeed in school might actually lead to a reversal of white flight; for most parents, the most powerful prejudice is not against children of a different race – it is their bias in favour of their own child's success. If sitting next to a South Asian or a Chinese-heritage child is the best way to improve a pupil's chances of academic achievement, I would be surprised to find any parent choosing the alternative.

To give society a clear view of where it stands, the government might consider the model successfully pioneered by the Social Mobility and Child Poverty Commission. This is a body with no enforcement powers; it is tiny – fewer than 20 employees. Yet, under the vigorous leadership of the former cabinet minister, Alan Milburn, the commission has produced a series of reports on social mobility that have galvanised Britain's professional bodies and universities into spending millions of pounds to widen their appeal beyond the products of public and selective schools. In the realm of integration, this is not a role that can easily be fulfilled by the EHRC, whose principal legal focus is equality, and which in recent years, has concerned itself less with matters of race and ethnicity. It should be a role for a completely new body.

Third, turning to the issue of offence, Parliament should take the opportunity in this administration to renew and formalise a presumption in favour of freedom of expression. It may be a matter for parliamentary draughtsmen to work out how this might be done; but there should be a case for the accretion of limitations and caveats on freedom of expression to be swept aside and replaced by legislation ensuring that only speech and gestures that directly encourage physical harm are subject to legal restriction.

In practice, this might mean that someone would be permitted to address me as 'nigger' – but they would be prohibited from pointing at me and telling their friends to 'go and get the nigger'. At a mundane level, it would, I hope discourage the growing practice of applying the term 'racist' to any individual or group whose views we find disagreeable, thus systematically degrading the force of the very word.

The next opportunity to consider this might be in the government's development of a new Bill of Rights. As unlikely as this is actually to take place, it may be that a Conservative administration would find it more palatable to take this task in parts, and to start with a revision to the law that would privilege a British version of Article 10. In the European Convention on Human Rights, this right is said to be 'qualified'. Its exercise should be 'proportionate', and can be limited by laws protecting 'health and morals' for example.[37] In a British bill of rights, such restraints should be removed.

Fourth, both openness of this degree and public scrutiny can only be achieved through the compilation, publication and analysis of relevant metrics. We could helpfully make a start by abandoning the baffling, backward-looking, black-and-white language of 'BMEs and BAMEs' in favour of the well understood and useful ONS categories. No-one knows what a BAME looks like, since the concept only exists in order to differentiate people by skin colour, rather than by attitudes, attainment, life-chances or anything else that really matters. In fact no-one even knows how to say the acronym; at a recent conference one speaker referred to 'bammys' throughout her presentation.

We could also start to tackle public and corporate anxiety about the topics of race and ethnicity by allowing the publication of more detailed data on what we describe as cultural 'ICE': the persistent effects on groups' behaviour of their inheritance, community norms and their environment, e.g. the nature of their neighbourhood. It is currently almost impossible to achieve this end, because most organisations believe that data protection legislation prevents them from keeping data about a person's race, ethnicity or religion, or indeed publishing any information that may reveal it. Even those who would like to use such information remain nervous about attributing a characteristic to an individual unless it is done with their permission. As a result, data on levels of integration is scarce and unreliable.

This is nonsense. At a common sense level, it is absurd to imagine that a characteristic which is immediately obvious (no-one who has seen a photograph of me imagines that I am white) can be anonymised in some fashion. At a technical level, the degree of non-response on tick-box forms makes the traditional process of collection of such data unreliable, with margins of error in the region of 25 per cent. Finally, as Richard Webber and I have shown, it is increasingly clear that the self-identification of ethnicity is all too often misleading if the aim is to understand or predict behavioural patterns, a principle which apples to subdivisions of white categories as much as it does to people of colour.[38] Clarification of this legislation would open the way to accurate and informative data for companies, charities and the public.

Conclusion

Superdiversity is presenting Britain with an extraordinary new challenge. We are not alone in this. But as we are seeing across the developed world, if we are to cope with societies that need new, different kinds of people to survive economically, we need to plan for the social consequences of change.

It is my view that the British tradition of 'organic' integration no longer meets the needs of our society. To continue to pursue it will lead to division and conflict, and undermine both equality and solidarity. In place of our laissez-faire attitude to integration, I believe we need something more directive and more muscular. This view will no doubt be contested. But to me, the choice is plain, both for dominant majorities and for minorities.

It is more urgent for minorities than anyone else. A society without realistic prospects of genuine integration is a society that, sooner or later, will give in to majority fears and prejudices. As the world speeds up we have less and less time to achieve a better balance.

In 1964 Dr Martin Luther King summoned up the vision of a young boy in Harlem, New York, and a young girl in Birmingham, Alabama, joining hands across hundreds of miles to fight for civil rights. King's vision, I would contend, has proven unequal to a new, globalised world, one far more complicated than he could have imagined. In the UK, our history is very different to his. But there is one thing we can learn from Dr King: his sense of urgency when it comes to tackling the issues of racial and ethnic difference. In his words:

> We are now faced with the fact that tomorrow is today. We are confronted with the fierce urgency of now... there is such a thing as being too late.

That is why, when it comes to meeting the integration challenge of the 21st century, again in King's language, we can't wait.

A Guide
Through the Maze

David Goodhart

This is a welcome compilation album pulling together Trevor Phillips's greatest hits on race and integration in Britain, with a few new numbers thrown in for good measure.

I have worked with Phillips on the Mapping Integration project (and the Integration Hub website) first at Demos and now at Policy Exchange and he has been a big influence on my own thinking so these comments are more of an elucidation than a critique.

The Phillips narrative here is an argument with what one might call '1980s anti-racism', a set of beliefs that he would once have subscribed to himself but which no longer adequately describe the world.

What does it assert? That ethnicity is largely skin-deep and white prejudice is the dominant experience of all non-whites (hence the binary white/non-white categorisations BME/BAME that he has been complaining about for some time).

It follows in this account that any departure from ethnic proportionality in educational or employment outcomes must be the result of systematic discrimination and if that discrimination is removed individuals will flourish, or not, according to their talents (or their social class inheritance) with ethnic and racial differences being revealed as no more important than hair colour.

What is the Phillips counter-narrative? In one of the most striking passages in the pamphlet he puts it like this:

> The problem is that in most western societies this simply hasn't turned out to be true. In fact, if anything the receding tide of post-war racial bigotry has simply exposed the jagged rocks of persistent cultural difference... Particularly here in the UK, we are having to face the fact that we are failing to cope with diversity; and that our historic experience of 20th century immigrant integration provides a poor template for the challenges of the 21st century.

He argues that the 'organic integration' that worked, more or less, for Huguenots, Jews, the Irish and even for the first waves of post-colonial immigration after the war required conditions that no longer pertain: a confident host society clear in its values and way of life, a manageable number of newcomers and time to absorb them.

Critics would no doubt claim that he provides scant evidence for the more recent failure of integration. But he has spelt out the details elsewhere—for example in his 2005 speech 'sleepwalking to segregation'. In any case two factoids suffice to suggest that some kind of polarisation, at least between the White British and the rest, is taking place: more than 40 per cent of visible minorities live in wards where they are the majority and more than half of visible minority school pupils go to schools where the White British are a minority. Instead of the mass creolisation that some people had expected by 2050 Britain (when the ethnic minority population will be at least one third) on current trends about half of all districts will look like today's London and half will be persistently White British.

This is in part a liberal failure, argues Phillips. A failure to see that as some minorities achieved a critical mass liberalism made it too easy to live apart (especially with the help of modern communications technologies). A failure too, thanks to the ideology of multiculturalism, to demand that newcomers adapt more to British ways. And Phillips is not shy about pointing to the self-inflicted wounds that make it harder for some minority groups to prosper and to the fact that many Muslims are resistant to the traditional process of integration—a small minority are even actively opposed to values that most Europeans take for granted.

(He does not dwell on the Muslim question in this pamphlet though one senses Muslim separation throughout. Similarly the word multiculturalism hardly appears at all, though the critique of it is everywhere, which is maybe Phillips practising what he preaches about the word now being merely a source of confusion. Misuse/overuse of the word racism gets short shrift too.)

Phillips is acutely aware of white liberal condescension and how the apparently progressive assumption that any minority failure must stem from unequal treatment by whites denies minority agency.

Indeed he may here underestimate the extent to which colonialism lies at the root of white liberal confusions and inhibitions about race. White liberals regard colonialism as Britain's original sin, like slavery in America, and multiculturalism as it developed in the 1970s and 1980s was seen as part of a new British mission to show the world that difference without domination could flourish in the mother country (see

Geoff Dench's *Minorities in the Open Society* which should be a better known book). But by cordoning off minorities in their own districts with their own leaders and social centres and making their progress dependent on white advocacy, white liberals were of course merely continuing the colonial heritage with a smiley face pasted on.

There are balancing acts here. Yes, ethnocultural background matters enormously and the data tells us that it currently produces very different outcomes for different groups. That is not, however, set in stone, nor an excuse for stereotyping or 'essentialism'—and everyone should still be treated as an individual citizen. To put it another way, because everyone should be treated equally does not mean everyone is the same.

So what is Phillips's 'active integration' answer to the failures of organic integration? One idea, that I expect Louise Casey's current government review of opportunity and integration to pick up, is to impose a legal duty on public bodies to promote integration. This may seem unduly statist for someone who emphasises the limits of the law in promoting progress here. But Phillips wants the duty to be applied with a light touch and through data transparency as much as anything: if all local authorities have to publish data about residential and school mix Bradford and Oldham will compete like crazy not to be bottom of the national integration league. That, anyway, is the hope.

I have a few quibbles. I think Phillips is a bit starry-eyed about Germany, which does not have a great record on integrating Turks. He also assumes that white parents will happily send their children to Indian or Chinese dominated schools because academic standards are so high. I don't think the record bears that out.

Most important, he underplays the interaction of class and ethnicity. If there are two things that stand in the way of greater cross-ethnic friendship and partnering, which is central to a well integrated society, it is class and religion. And in the most divided places in Britain, the Yorkshire and Lancashire mill towns, the dominant minority – Kashmiri Pakistanis – are separated from the British mainstream by both. (Incidentally, looks are over-rated. Your fellow citizens are people who sound like you, not people who look like you.)

As the American writer Michael Lind has put it:

> If you get rid of formal racism but don't churn the classes you have a de facto racialised class system even if nobody is a racist... Thus all those Latin American countries with one culture but light skinned elites and dark skinned masses. And in both the US and Brazil you have the class legacy of white supremacy and slavery which is best addressed by race neutral social mobility and education policies not racial preferences that infuriate those who don't qualify.

(It might be interesting to consider the extent to which the Anglo-American concern with home ownership exacerbates the segregation problem, with people acutely sensitive to whether the arrival of outsiders into a neighbourhood might reduce the value of their property and thus their main source of family wealth.)

Why does all this matter? Given how important ethnicity remains to both minorities and majorities (look at the extent of white flight) what is wrong with some degree of separation? Is peaceful co-existence – separate but equal with some mixing and inter-marriage at the margins – really such a terrible thing?

It is hard to challenge such complacency about segregation because it depends on judgments about how things are going to turn out in a few decades' time. Phillips argues that if we allow things to drift in the current direction it will lead to a white backlash. I think that is unlikely, my anxiety is more fundamental: that we will cease to think as one society with at least some common interests; the public sphere will become balkanised and the welfare state will shrivel as our sense of solidarity becomes reserved only for people like us.

But in the here and now there is also, thanks in part to Phillips himself, a growing political consensus that if a good society is one that acknowledges ethnic difference but also experiences thick traffic across class and ethnic boundaries in the name of common citizenship then we have a problem in many parts of the country. Weakening the linguistic, religious, class and residential obstacles to integration is a huge project that will not happen through state intervention but nor will it happen on its own. Fortunately we have in David Cameron the first Conservative prime minister who seems genuinely interested in the issue and we also have Phillips to guide us – and him, I hope – through the maze.

Immigrants Come From Somewhere (Else)

Jon Gower Davies

As his rather ominous original title showed (*Race: The Silence of the Damned*), Trevor Phillips imagines greater dangers ahead.* His essay abounds in minatory words: *time-bomb, disaster, danger, microaggression, pernicious, crisis, catastrophe*. May I say at the outset that I do not agree with this: or rather that while I do think there are dangers ahead, this is not for the reasons Mr Phillips gives. He is still, I think, mired in the ideology of multiculturalism, and so perhaps unable to see that 'race', in its 'multi-varieties' is no great matter. What is likely to make the lives of my children and grandchildren dangerous and perhaps catastrophic, is religion, indeed one religion, Islam, and its adherents, Muslims: and to this issue I will return later.

For some decades Trevor Phillips has been one of the leaders of the Britain-based multi-cultural ideology. While I infer from this latest piece of writing that he is now having not so much second as superimposed thoughts, I have difficulty in seeing much that might help solve the problems to which his earlier promotional activity has given rise. His analysis of the

---

* Editor's note: *Race: The Silence of the Damned* had been Trevor Phillips' working title, attached to the draft on which David Goodhart and Jon Gower Davies were asked to comment. It was amended before final publication.

promise and problems of 'superdiversity' and 'social solidarity' is perhaps a bit misleading. May I also say that, over and above the demographics of 'multiculturalism' (not to my mind much of a problem) we have the more serious problems caused by the ideology of multiculturalism, which under the loud voice of 'tolerance' has so muted our intelligence as to make us blind to, indeed indulgent of, one very serious danger. This is the legacy given us by the ideologues of multiculturalism, amongst whom we must include Mr Phillips and his Equality and Human Rights Commission (EHRC), his colleague and associate Lord Parekh and his report of 2000, and Sir William Macpherson and his report of 1999.

Even so, I would not blame these gentlemen and their collective ideology for the larger problems we face in Great Britain, problems which will indeed tax to the limit my children and grandchildren. We have become what we are through our own (misguided) efforts. Multiculturalism simply gives us one more problem to deal with (and in some sense gives us some resource as well as problem). And while I comment critically on Mr Phillips's essay, it is also the case that I welcome it and the semi-truths it contains.

State and Society – State or Society?

The distinction between these two is a basic assumption of British liberalism and libertarian practice: and I am not sure that Mr Phillips understands this. My doubts about this are perhaps exemplified in his reference to what he claims to be his leading role in destroying the British National Party. He seems to be saying that he used the tax-derived resources of the EHRC to sue the BNP into non-existence:

> There is no significant far-right or nativist force in
> our politics; in January 2016 the noxious BNP
> quietly slipped out of existence, crippled by internal
> feuding and financial debt (mostly brought about, I
> am pleased to say, by legal action I took as chairman
> of the Equality and Human Rights Commission).

We can perhaps set aside Phillips's grasp of current British politics, such an erroneous claim, such a boast. To have used a tax-based state institution to destroy a political party – if this is what he did – highlights a worrying misunderstanding of who we are and how we might order our politics and re-cast 'our' 'management' of the sundry mini-cultures now resident here.

Students like me were brought up on Hobbes, Locke, Burke and Thomas Jefferson – and later Max Weber and Isaiah Berlin. I have all my life been grounded in such theorists, as well as in my case in John Milton, The Bible and moralists such as John Wesley. From this admittedly polyglot collection, I/we derived one very clear premise: that there is and should be a clear distinction between the range and scope of the State and the range and scope of Civil Society; and that the operative assumption should be that the range and scope of the State, i.e. of compulsion, should be progressively and carefully narrowly defined, while to Civil Society, the locus of voluntariness and liberty, should be allocated more and more of the serious purpose of the nation. The underlying assumption is that things done voluntarily will endure, while things done in obedience to authority will wither and vanish once that authority has gone.

The powers of the State are legitimate only when it operates impartially. Perhaps I should say: in a democracy, the powers of the State are legitimate only when it operates impartially.

If the State is all, then Society is nothing.

If Society is all, then in the absence of a shared value system, and a clear moral border, then chaos and conflict break out. Multiculturalism has pushed more and more aspects of life away from the voluntary (Society) into the realm of compulsion (the State), thereby weakening and corrupting both.

Mr Phillips's new model multiculturalism

The multiculturalism of which Mr Phillips was once a leading proponent 'pushed' more and more of the business of Society into the hands of the State, i.e. of compulsion. Worse, under the plausible admonitions of multiculturalism, the State 'takes sides' and intrudes into the business of Society. The gap between the two is transgressed, to the corruption of both.

Some years ago I wrote a short book (*A New Inquisition: religious persecution in Britain today*) in which I described the deployment of six police officers and a detective chief inspector and the relevant personnel of the Crown Prosecution Service to take to a Liverpool court two hotel keepers who had taken part, in the hotel foyer, in a discussion/debate with a Muslim guest about the respective merits of Islam and Christianity. The guest complained. While the judge threw the case out, the hoteliers were bankrupted. At the time I wrote this book there were in existence 35 Acts of Parliament, 52 Statutory Instruments, 13 Codes of Practice, three Codes of Guidance and 16 European Commission Directives which made it illegal to 'hate' anyone because of their race, colour, ethnic origin, nationality, national origin, religion, lack of religion, gender, gender identity, sexual orientation, disability, age, etc. Rousseau would no doubt see this as good practice – forcing us to be free of hate.

This confusion of the divide between State and Civil Society corrupts both. Phillips is aware of this, saying for example that he would now regard being called a nigger, no matter how unpleasant, as a matter for societal concern (i.e. his own business) and not that of the State. No more, he says, referring to the French law prohibiting the niqab, should the state tell a woman how to dress. Phillips, however, stressing (as I do) the need for 'social solidarity', cannot resist reverting to loading the busy-body state with the 'duties' required, he says, for such a purpose. Thus, for example, he says that the concerns about a small number of Muslim and Sikh schools are 'wrong and disproportionate': but he then goes on to make things worse. 'Policy', he says, 'should focus on the places where almost all majority children attend' as well as nine out of 10 minority children. The 'duty to integrate' he is calling for should, he says, apply to minority faith schools as well as to an exclusive public school, so that they can all demonstrate that they make efforts to give their pupils 'a real experience of living in a diverse society'. Further, such a

> duty should apply to charities as well as public bodies. This would mean that places of worship, both majority and minority, might be required to show the Charity Commissioner that they are making 'real efforts to open their doors to believers and non-believers'. Such a duty applied in this way would, he feels, 'challenge the practice being urged on Sikh gurdwaras to prohibit the marriage of Sikhs to non-Sikhs'.

True, he says that such a duty should be enforced 'lightly', and that while the duty to integrate 'should be applied with some force to educational institutions', 'none of this 'should be subject to any enforcement regime other than that provided by the market'. He urges Parliament to draft a document 'in favour of freedom of expression', as if this would compensate for the loss of such freedom implicit in the various 'hate' laws.

Yet in offering comment on educational and other institutions, the old regulator re-emerges. While urging the elaboration of the new 'duty to integrate', he says that he 'would not propose the removal of the positive equality duties on public bodies, cumbersome and bureaucratic as they are'. The new duty would thus be an addition to the array of restrictions. There is, he says, neither the time to wait for a 'natural convergence' nor, 'in a globalised world, with the aggressive proselytising of Islamist militancy can we rely on the notion that every community will, with time, come to see the value and attractiveness of western values and ways of living'.

What underlies the evident confusion in such an analysis? Partly, the old tendency of the old multiculturalism to see as 'discriminatory' any policy which does not apply *to everyone* – to all minorities and to the majority: this is rather like pre-emptive fining of everyone just because someone has broken or may break the law. So, following this logic, we now have proposals for Ofsted to 'inspect' Christian Sunday Schools and out-of-hours church-related activities just so that some religious activities, which may indeed most definitely need 'inspection', do not feel that they are being 'discriminated' against. Needless to say, an 'inspection' regime so extended will inevitably become less efficient than one focused on a real and more clearly defined target: a supervision of everyone means an adequate supervision of no one: and any bureaucrat carrying out his or her duties 'lightly' will soon be summoned to answer a charge of 'institutional indolence', while a bureaucrat showing greater vigour will be accused of 'institutional arrogance'.

Islam and Muslims: the real problem

Mr Phillips refers to 'Islamist terrorism now being firmly camped on our own European shores'. The term 'Islamist', of course, is used to avoid the more direct 'Islamic', thus preserving the basic apologetic that 'Islam is a religion of peace' and that the run-of-the mill Muslim would no more subscribe to such violence than would the run-of-the mill Sikh or Hindu or Roman Catholic.

Indeed, on several occasions Mr Phillips equates Muslims and Sikhs – when, for example, problems in 'a tiny number of schools' are described as being Muslim and Sikh, and Sikh gurdwaras being oppressive. The Sikh 'threat' is as nothing compared to the threat embedded in our Muslim communities.

This is the standard multicultural dogma, implicit in the use of the term 'Islamist'. Mr Phillips gets half way to the truth: and there is clearly little need for me to say, here, much more than this: that Muslim antipathy or hostility towards the West is rooted in much more than simply being a minority on our shores or in the demographics of their communities.

As I understand it, Mr Phillips is asking us now to consider that how incoming minorities behave is more the expression of where they come from and who they are, rather than the result of oppression and discrimination by the native majority. He is, now, on the right track, though still showing signs of camouflaging the real problem.

The demographic time-bomb

What 'demographic time-bomb'? There are about 1.5 billion Muslims in the world: and about 30 million Sikhs. On its own, this makes Phillips's 'partnering' of Sikhs and Muslims rather odd. The spread of Muslims through the world on its *own* goes some way to guarantee that there will be, and is, conflict within the Muslim world and between it and the West. Television news programmes and newspapers attest to this on a daily basis.

More parochially, we have a 'demographic time-bomb' of sorts in our prisons. In this case, comparisons are useful and enlightening.

There are about 500,000 Sikhs in the UK, and about 700,000 Hindus. Criminal Sikhs in the prisons of England and Wales number 777 and criminal Hindus number 456. Thus together, they provide 1,233 prisoners in the prisons of England Wales: and if you add Buddhists and Jews to this, these minorities provide 3,241 prisoners (of which, to my surprise, Buddhists account for 1,756). Muslims on their own provide 11,248, being 13 per cent of the prison population – well above their due statistical 'share' – and growing.[1]

The usual *apologetic* for this crime wave is forthcoming. In commenting on the increasing numbers of Muslim prisoners, Muzammil Quraishi, senior lecturer in criminology and criminal justice at Salford University, said: 'Young Muslim men are under the official gaze from their school days onwards – they have the lens of the state turned on them. Certain populations can become suspect in the eyes of the law enforcement agencies.' Mizanur Rahman of the organisation Muslim Prisoners blamed the increase on Islamophobia and racism among police officers.[2]

This of course is the standard multicultural apologetic: blame the majority. I do not know Dr Quraishi, senior lecturer at a British university: nor Mr Rahman of Muslim Prisoners: but this mobilisation of denial-defence is very typical. In my book of 2009 *In Search of the Moderate Muslim* I suggested that we should avoid terms such as 'Islamism' or theological terms such as 'Islam': and operate on the assumption that Islam is what Muslims do. This gives us a kind of sociology of the Muslim presence in the United Kingdom. In the UK alone, there are currently 3,000 Muslims under surveillance by the security services. As we have seen, there are about 12-13,000 Muslim convicts at various times being fed back into and out of 'the' Muslim community/ies.

Research by Marie Macey (detailed in my book) shows how powerful these criminals are in their 'communities': and, more recently, an article in the *Daily Mail* shows that the force of Muslim violence is maintained in prison, where their activities both strengthen their own allegiances and force them on others.[3] For this reason, the prime minister suggested having separate jails for such Muslims!

Surveys show that about 20-25 per cent of 'British Muslims' support the use of violence – that's about 500,000 people. On the rare occasion when members of 'the' community contact the security services about a relative who has gone to, say, Syria, it is usually because they/the family are concerned about the safety of their relatives, not because they fundamentally disagree with what they intend to do. After Paris, the threat of Muslim violence on our streets has, for example, led to the number of armed police being doubled. This is not because of Sikhs demonstrating against a theatre or Hindus supporting the BJP on the streets of the UK.

As I said, Muslim antipathy or hostility is rooted in much more than demographics.

In essence, while we Brits once had an empire of which we are now ashamed, Muslims once had an empire which they are ashamed to have lost and to the restoration of which they aspire.

Their distance from or their antipathy to us is not because of what or who we are but *because of what we are not* – we are 'not Muslim'. A conversation with the Council of Ex-Muslims of Britain will tell you what this means. It means zero 'conversion' to 'our' way of life. The major Muslim organisations are exercises in apologetics and camouflage – see the above quotations – further re-inforcing the distance between us, a distance written into Muslim history and self-conception. So, for example, some years ago I wrote, in *In Search of the Moderate Muslim*, a chapter entitled 'We are the Fascists who Won'. This I intended ironically. I thought that no reasonable person could really think that us white Brits, conquerors of fascism, are all Hitlers. Yet more recently, and to my horror, I read in *Winning the Modern World for Islam*, by Abdessalem Yassine, that 'Hitler's war... is nothing but the decisive manifestation of a modern notion of progress founded on reason and committed entirely to efficiency'.

We are, it seems, of one piece with Hitler and his policies. Islam is indeed a singular and very serious problem, and should not be considered under the general rubric of multiculturalism, whether as it was or as now revised by Mr Phillips. Islam is not susceptible to multicultural blandishments. And contrary to his opinion, that this is a 'small minority' actively opposed to European values, Muslims are a large and growing 'demographic' incapable of setting aside their dis-relish for who we are.

Further, Muslims, it seems to me, have never been at ease or at peace with Islam (no more than Christians have with Christianity). Indeed, from the time of its arrival in the world, Muslims have lived and live in a permanent state of civil war: and as there are so many of them, this civil war is a global conflict, a war in our world too, carried on in a social expanse we, the West, have created: freedom's empty space.

Without Muslims 'the UK problem' would be soluble. With them, Mr Phillips' 'duty to integrate' is a joke – a tragic joke, for sure. It is the duty of the State to ensure that this particular 'joke' does not explode in our faces. The rest, the matters of 'race' to which Mr Phillips refers in his title, can be left to the slow but sure ministrations of Civil Society, suitably freed from the detritus of multicultural laws and structures, left to the slow blandishments of freedom.

Too late?

As Phillips is aware, the demography of Great Britain is now such that it will never again be the unified society in which I grew up. When I travel down to Newcastle from Orkney I pass over or through a Scotland which has already left the UK, no matter what the referendum said. Going South to Newcastle and 'Tyne and Wear', we see urban areas which are essentially museum pieces, kept alive by public expenditure. In the Midlands, we enter the 'Great Northern Powerhouse', and we find cities like Birmingham with a non-white British population getting on for half. The aim of the proposed huge rail connection is to turn this Midland zone into a suburb of London. London is already a 'world city', with over half its population born somewhere other than the UK: two of my children live there – and love it. Many young people, whites leading, tend to move out into the surrounding counties of rural England. Some 300,000 people leave the UK every year.

There is no reversing this demography through the agency of the State. Slowly, through voluntary spontaneous co-operative action and self-interest, many, perhaps most, of the people so assembled will develop some kind of shared culture. When I go with my daughter to take her children to the nearby school, I can see that it is already happening. This is the best we can hope for.

Slavery: Us, the majority v minorities?

Why is the Muslim world so incompatible with ours? Are they alone in this, or are Hindus, Sikhs, Buddhists also ill at ease with our culture and values system? Some 50 or so years ago, in the summer of 1964, I was part of the Student Non-Violent Coordinating Committee (SNNC) campaign to get the black people of Mississippi registered to vote. As I walked down a street in a small town in Mississippi two (white) men in a truck tried to run me over, to kill me. A complaint to the (white) sheriff simply elicited a gun waved in my face. Three of our fellow volunteers had already disappeared, killed, it turned out, by other members of the (white) law 'enforcement' establishment.

Why this level of hate, I asked myself. In the American South, of course, it must have had something to do with 'slavery' and the agony of its abolition one hundred years before, in America's bloodiest war.

Going back in time, I grew up in colonial Kenya, so the violence of race and tribal hatred was not new to me. Human beings create and live within hierarchies of institutionalised political cruelty, exclusion and predation. I do not know why they do this and I do know that this is not all that they do: but do it they do. Slavery defines the moral nadir of and basis for all such systems of predatory humanity-corroding hierarchies. It is, as John Wesley said, 'the execrable sum of all villainies' (Cowherd, 47) giving birth to and/or validating ancillary bigotries of all kinds – racisms, serfdoms, the degradation of women, sexual exploitation, rape and homophobia, the oppressions of caste and of class – all the hideous pompous nastiness of human segregations and demeaning – the all-powerful primal corrosive out-reach of slavery. It seemed to me that to begin to erode and ostracise both slavery and its hydra-headed ancillary systems, only a culture which has from within itself generated 'autochthonously', an effective anti-slavery morality will prove able to procreate and ferry – albeit unsteadily – the increasing boon and burdens of hierarchy-corrosive notions of human (including gender) equality, freedom, individualism, democracy, the rule of law and the elaboration of human rights. Such notions are the very expression of the erosion of predatory restrictive hierarchies, necessarily starting with and including the erosion of the prior and most primeval one, slavery: and then follows, or can follow, the nullification of abhorrent hierarchies and the gradual pacification of power-politics. The spontaneous ending of slavery is the absolutely necessary condition for this journey into the world of freedoms.

For the 200 or so nation states of the world we have now a broad and comprehensive set of international surveys which tell us what life is like in the countries from which our immigrants come. It is hard to find in any of their histories an autochthonous removal of slavery: more often than not it was eliminated by external powers, the British especially: and perhaps here we can get some reason for the various forms of radical inegalitarianisms evinced by, for example, people from Pakistan or India or Bangladesh. Their cultures come with them. They are not created by oppressions visited upon them by their hosts.

Do rights eliminate gratitude?

In conclusion, I quote Jena, the mother of Muslim activist and journalist Yasmin Alibhai-Brown. The family came here from Uganda, fleeing the hostility of Idi Amin. Jena is now dead, but she said this to her critically-minded daughter:

> ...show respect to the old citizens of Britain for sharing their small island with us... Things were better than under Amin... Look what they have given me – a pension, my own independence... I know you are fighting for equality but life is not perfect.

Wisdom wiser by far than the lengthy complaint of multiculturalism.

Reflections

Trevor Phillips

Both Jon Gower Davies and David Goodhart treat the topic of modern superdiversity with the utmost seriousness, even if they don't wholly transfer that respect to my arguments. That's appreciated. I think we all agree on the need, in the words of the former Chief Rabbi, Jonathan Sacks,

> to think again about what it is to be human in the company of others in a world full of danger and diversity.[1]

However, if we are to think together, it may pay us to listen more closely to what we are each saying. In reading Jon Gower Davies' response, I wondered if, as often still happens, he had confused me with someone else (usually, Sir Trevor McDonald, or more recently, the Radio 1 DJ Trevor Nelson). I doubt if anyone else would describe me as 'mired in the ideology of multiculturalism'. More people would point the finger at me as the man who murdered it.

Perhaps we are more at one on the question of the challenge posed by Islam – though I disagree with what Jon implies, that Islam cannot flourish in Europe. My take is that faced with a religion unused to having its adherents form a small minority in a society, we all have to work much harder than in the past to find a way of achieving Berlin's aim of living together graciously.

This is not just a problem for Muslims to solve. If anything it is a tension felt even more acutely by our deracinated political and media classes. For many in our liberal white elite who have cast aside their own roots as Catholics or Jews (for example), in favour of a kind of anaemic atheism, it must be profoundly discomfiting to encounter a group of people, who are in most ways exactly like themselves – doctors, lawyers, academics and journalists – yet who resolutely refuse to renounce the values and practice of their everyday faith.

The answer for many non-Muslim liberals appears to be to comfort themselves by asserting that they (British Muslims) are only pretending for the sake of their parents; or worse still 'they'll get over it', because at heart we're all the same, and in time they'll see that 'our' ways are better. The thing is – they're not pretending, won't get over it and we aren't all the same. Moreover, we don't have the time to wait around for elite opinion to catch up with reality.

David Goodhart flatters me by suggesting that these are my 'greatest hits'. But his proposition that Britain's current shyness over ethnocultural difference stems from its embarrassment over its colonial past strikes a chord. The recent student posturing over statues, supported by many in the faculty, does suggest that colonialism has taken on the mantle of original sin in some way. This would merit some further investigation by people better qualified than I am.

This is even more true of David's barb that I – in effect – dodged the issue of 'class'. I don't think that this is wholly fair. My view, which perhaps isn't adequately articulated, is that we have to move on from the social democratic assumption that almost all important racial disadvantage not deriving from straightforward bigotry should be attributed to what people call class, and measured by socio-economic indicators. I simply don't agree that we should regard race and ethnicity just as functions of socio-economic status and not as independent variables. Middle class black and brown folk, for example, suffer penalties which are nothing to do with their parents' or their own income and everything to do with their parents' colour and culture.

To be fair to David, since he read this essay we published the new work about viewing of terrestrial TV channels which appears in this essay. In theory, since terrestrial TV channels are all equally available and the choice of popular programming is pretty much impervious to most factors including income, the gap in viewing patterns suggests that it is culture and race that differentiates, not class.

All that said, I do think that David has a point. There is much more that we should be able to understand about the interaction between race and class. In the United States, there are inconclusive experiments being undertaken to limit the socio-economic mix of schools in the hope of raising standards for all groups. We have yet to see the results.

One of my own nagging, unresolved worries here concerns the ethnic hierarchy of educational attainment – which is almost an exact inversion of the level of interethnic marriage. African Caribbeans, notoriously and chronically underachieving, have been most likely to marry White Brits, whilst Hindu Indians, who have tended to marry co-ethnics, are consistently at the other end of the attainment scale. The correspondence isn't exact, but I think there must be a question about whether the immigrants who are most likely to mix with the least successful white groups are also likely to adopt their behaviours – including low educational aspirations and chaotic family patterns. Does a lack of integration provide a kind of cultural insulation against underclass behaviours? And are we in danger of creating a new caste system which combines the worst of class – and race-based inequalities?

I don't know the answer. But sooner rather than later, a superdiverse society has to understand and solve these problems. It will do so noisily and fractiously or not at all. The alternative is to achieve tranquility by the route favoured by virtually every dictator and empire in recorded history – by stamping out all that awkward human diversity, and with it, all of the creative tensions that have driven human progress since we gathered round the campfire to quarrel about the best way to divide the day's hunt.

The greatest dangers to the continued vigour and prosperity of our diverse society are to bury our real differences under a veneer of sham courtesy; and to patronise minorities by treating us as groups who, if protected by liberal opinion and afforded the right tutelage, might one day qualify to become honorary whites. So dial down the anxiety about diversity, ignore the angst about Islamophobia. Superdiversity calls out for honest and open speech. There is bound to be some pain along the way. But just as the heat of a burning candle teaches us the limits of our physical tolerance, we need to embrace offence as the price we pay for a better, more vibrant, more modern society.

Notes

Race and Faith: The Deafening Silence
Trevor Phillips

1   Klein, J., 'Why Race and Tribe Trump Economics In The Current Presidential Campaign', *Time*, January 18, 2016.

2   Vertovec, S., 'Super-diversity and its Implications', *Ethnic and Racial Studies*, Vol 30 Issue 6, 2005, pp.1024-1054.

3   Phillips, T., 'Superdiversity: Television's Newest Reality', 2008: http://www.coe.int/t/dg4/cultureheritage/mars/source/resources/references/others/48%20-%20Superdiversity%20Television's%20newest%20reality%20-%20Philipps%202008.pdf

4   Phillips, T., 'I Won't Join The Letwin Lynch Mob', *The Observer*, January 3, 2016: http://www.theguardian.com/commentisfree/2016/jan/03/i-wont-join-anti-letwin-lynch-mob

5   StatistischesBundesamt: https://www.destatis.de/EN/PressServices/Press/pr/2015/04/PE15_153_12421.html

6   Carlqvist, I., and L. Hedegaard, 'Sweden: Rape Capital of the West': http://www.gatestoneinstitute.org/5195/sweden-rape

7   Goodhart, D., Integration Hub: http://www.integrationhub.net/module/education/

8   Sunak, R., and S. Rajeswaran, 'A Portrait of Modern Britain', Policy Exchange, 2014.

9   Ibid.

10 Stone, J., 'Another 3 million refugees and migrants will arrive in Europe in 2016', *The Independent*, November 5, 2015: http://www.independent.co.uk/news/world/europe/eu-expecting-another-3-million-refugees-migrants-before-end-of-2016-a6722096.html

11 Sunak and Rajeswaran.

12 Nawaz, M., 'Why The Survey of British Muslim Attitudes Is So Profoundly Disconcerting', *The Independent*, February 25, 2015: http://www.independent.co.uk/voices/comment/why-the-survey-of-british-muslim-attitudes-is-so-profoundly-disconcerting-10070358.html

13 Full text: 'Enoch Powell's "Rivers of Blood" Speech', *The Daily Telegraph*, November 6, 2007: http://www.telegraph.co.uk/comment/3643823/Enoch-Powells-Rivers-of-Blood-speech.html

14 Bartholomew, J., 'The awful rise of "virtue signalling"', *The Spectator*, April 18, 2015: http://www.spectator.co.uk/2015/04/hating-the-daily-mail-is-a-substitute-for-doing-good/

15 Channel 4 News, March 12, 2015: http://www.channel4.com/news/nigel-farage-race-discrimination-laws-scrapped

16 'Transgender Equality', The Women and Equlities Committee, House of Commons, January 8, 2016 http://www.publications.parliament.uk/pa/cm201516/cmselect/cmwomeq/390/390.pdf

17 Phillips, T., 'Ten Things About Race That Are True But We Can't Say', *The Sunday Times*, March 15, 2015 http://www.thesundaytimes.co.uk/sto/newsreview/features/article1530667.ece

18 Hewstone, M., et al., various studies. See: http://www.psy.ox.ac.uk/research/the-oxford-centre-for-the-study-of-intergroup-conflict-oxcsic

19 Phillips, M., and T., Phillips, *Windrush : The Irresistible Rise of Multi-Racial Britain*, London, Harper Collins, 2009.

20 https://www.ipsos-mori.com/Assets/Docs/Publications/sri-perceptions-and-reality-immigration-report-summary-2013.pdf

21 https://www.ipsos-mori.com/Assets/Docs/Publications/sri-perceptions-and-reality-immigration-report-summary-2013.pdf

22 MacArthur, Brian (ed.), *The Penguin Book of Twentieth-Century Speeches*, London, Penguin Books, 2000.

23 Ture, K., and C. Hamilton, *Black Power: The Politics of Liberation*, 1967.

24 http://ec.europa.eu/justice/discrimination/files/burden_of_proof_en.pdf

25 ONS, '2011 Census Analysis: How do Living Arrangements, Family Type and Family Size Vary in England and Wales?': http://webarchive.nationalarchives.gov.uk/20160105160709/http://www.ons.gov.uk/ons/rel/census/2011-census-analysis/how-do-living-arrangements--family-type-and-family-size-vary-in-england-and-wales-/story-on-how-do-living-arrangements--family-type-and-family-size-vary-in-england-and-wales-.html#tab-Family-types-by-country-of-birth

26 Phillips, T., 'British Media: Not Quite Black and White': https://www.opendemocracy.net/ourbeeb/trevor-phillips/british-tv-not-quite-black-and-white

27 The NSMC Showcase, 'Getting The Right Treatment': http://www.nsmcentre.org.uk/sites/default/files/Getting%20 the%20Right%20Treatment%20FULL%20benchmark%20case%2 0study.pdf

28 The Behavioural Insights Team, 'Update Report 2013-2015', London, 2015: http://www.behaviouralinsights.co.uk/wp-content/uploads/2015/07/BIT_Update-Report-Final-2013-2015 .pdf

29 Department for Education, 'GCSE and Equivalent Attainment By Pupil Characteristics In England 2012/13': https:// www.gov.uk/government/uploads/system/uploads/attachme nt_data/file/280689/SFR05_2014_Text_FINAL.pdf

30 Johnston, R., S. Burgess, D. Wilson and R. Harris, 'School and Residential Ethnic Segregation: An Analysis of Variations Across England's Local Education Authorities', *Regional Studies*, Vol 40, Issue 9, 2006, pp. 973-990.

31 Commission on Inequality in Education, 'Educational Inequalities in England and Wales', Social Market Foundation: http://www.smf.co.uk/wp-content/uploads/2016/01/Publication -Commission-on-Inequality-in-Education-Initial-Findings-Slide-Pack-120116.pdf

32 Burgess, S., 'Understanding The Success of London's Schools', Working Paper 14/333 CMPO University of Bristol, 2014: http://www.bristol.ac.uk/media-library/sites/cmpo/migrated/ documents/wp333.pdf

33 http://www.ncbi.nlm.nih.gov/pmc/articles/PMC3209820/; http://www.ncbi.nlm.nih.gov/pubmed/22002644

34 Street, R., et al., 'Understanding Concordance in Patient-Physician Relationships: Personal and Ethnic Dimensions of Shared Identity', Annals of Family Medicine, May 2008, pp.198-205: http://www.ncbi.nlm.nih.gov/pmc/articles/PMC2384992/

35 *Food Statistics Pocketbook 2015*, Defra, London, 2016: https://www.gov.uk/government/uploads/system/uploads/ attachment_data/file/461296/foodpocketbook-2015report-17sep15.pdf

36 Goodhart, D., *The British Dream: Successes and Failures of Post-War Immigration*, London, Atlantic Books, 2014.

37 https://www.liberty-human-rights.org.uk/human-rights/what-are-human-rights/human-rights-act/article-10-freedom-expression

38 Webber, R., and T. Phillips, 'Scotland's Many Subcultures', *Demos Quarterly*, July 18, 2014.

Immigrants Come From Somewhere (Else)
Jon Gower Davies

1   Berman, G., and A. Dar, 'Prison Population Statistics', House of Commons Library Note (SN/SG/4334), July 29, 2013.

2   Morris, N., 'Number of Muslims in prison doubles in decade to 12,000', *The Independent*, March 28, 2014.

3   Rawstorne, T., 'The Muslim extremists taking over British jails', *Daily Mail*, February 15, 2016.

4   Alibhai-Brown, Y., *The Settler's Cookbook: A Memoir of Love, Migration and Food*, Portobello Books, 2008, p.423.

Reflections
Trevor Phillips

1   Sacks, J., 'The Quest for a Moral Compass', *The Tablet*, April 24, 2014: http://www.thetablet.co.uk/books/10/2178/the-quest-for-a-moral-compass-a-global-history-of-ethics